Practical Test
for car drivers

Published by BSM
in association with
Virgin Books

New edition published in the UK in 2008 by
The British School of Motoring Ltd
8 Surrey Street
Norwich
Norfolk NR1 3NG

ISBN: 978-0-7535-1392-7
Designed by Thalamus Publishing
Printed in Italy

In the quote on the front cover: *A pass every
two minutes is calculated using 2007 pass
statistics and standard test centre opening
hours.

Contents

Foreword

Driving is an enjoyable and useful lifetime experience. That is why almost a million new learner drivers take to the road every year, each with one clear ambition – to pass their driving test first time.

Of course, there is no substitute for practical experience when learning to drive, and the best way to gain this is by taking lessons with a good professional driving instructor who uses the most up-to-date teaching techniques in a modern, dual-controlled car. However, to get the most out of your lessons it is important to prepare and take advantage of extra driving experience beyond your lessons with an accompanying driver and this book will help you in that – not just for the test, but for a lifetime of safe driving. There are no short cuts to becoming a safe and competent motorist.

So, make sure you have enough experience behind the wheel and that you are fully aware of the rules of the road. Practical Test for car drivers will help you to develop your driving skills and ensure that what you learn during the course of your lessons will lay the foundations for the way you drive for the rest of your life.

In over 90 years of teaching people to drive, BSM instructors have helped millions of people pass their driving test. With every new skill it is important to gain as much practice as possible. Throughout your driving life you will experience many driving scenarios on all types of road and weather conditions, so gaining as much experience as you can in the early stages will help you become prepared not only to pass your test first time, but also for a lifetime of safer driving.

This book has been developed to help you through your learning in a structured way, so that you can keep a track of your progress and work with your instructor and an accompanying driver to create a complete learning package. This way all three of you can work together to ensure that you are well prepared for your test and pass first time.

In my view, Practical Test for car drivers is the best book available to help you make the most of your driving lessons and ensure that you approach your Practical Test in a structured and positive way.

Robin Cummins OBE
Road Safety Consultant

Robin Cummins is one of Britain's leading authorities on motoring and driver education. He was formally the Chief Driving Examiner for the Driving Standards Agency having responsibility for driving tests and Approved Driving Instructor standards.

professional manner, and, while also having the authority to refuse or end a lesson early, abide by the law and not discriminate against any learner

☐ have the highest standards of personal conduct during the lesson, including:

   ■ courteous and considerate service

   ■ avoidance of physical contact except in an emergency

   ■ not smoking during any training

   ■ restricting mobile phone calls to emergencies and those for your benefit

☐ provide a presentable, modern, properly maintained, dual-controlled car on every lesson

☐ always endeavour to be on time at the agreed meeting point, and be available for the full duration of the lesson, subject to unforeseen circumstances beyond your instructor's control

☐ endeavour to give you two working days' (excluding weekends and Bank Holidays) notice should a lesson need to be rescheduled subject to circumstances beyond your instructor's control

☐ respond professionally to any worries or issues which you may have, trying to resolve them to your satisfaction or, if appropriate, offer the name of the BSM Business Manager to whom the matter should ultimately be referred in writing

☐ participate in our quality programme to ensure a consistent standard of teaching.

Your Track Record

Your Track Record is a tool for you and your instructor to keep a record of your theory and driving progress. It is based on the official Learning To Drive syllabus and identifies all the skills you need to drive safely. It will help your instructor to individually tailor your programme of lessons to suit you, so you should make sure you have your Track Record with you on every lesson.

There are 45 driving skills, each with five assessment levels. Your instructor will introduce each skill as appropriate. There is no set order and your instructor will assess when to introduce each skill. This could depend on:

❑ your progress

❑ the area where you learn

❑ the time you take your lessons (with regard to the road, traffic and weather conditions)

As you progress, your instructor will fill in the date and level reached for each individual skill. But remember, levels can go down as well as up!

You can check your own progress and review how you are getting on.

Preparing to learn

Your licence

You want to learn to drive and are excited at the prospect – so you probably can't wait to get started. However, before you can actually sit behind the wheel, there are a few things you must do to stay legal. The minimum age at which you are normally allowed to drive a car on the public roads is 17. If you are disabled and in receipt of mobility allowance, 16 is the minimum age.

Until the day when you pass the practical part of your driving test, you are not allowed to drive on your own. You must be accompanied by a person who is over 21 years of age and who has held a full British driving licence, valid for the type of vehicle you wish to drive, for a minimum of three years.

Before you start to drive, you must obtain a provisional driving licence. You can get an application form from the Post Office. You will need to include a passport-type photo for identification purposes. You may not drive until you have received your licence, which consists of two parts.

Check out: www.direct.gov.uk for information on applying for a licence.

Before you drive, you must also make sure that your eyesight meets the minimum standard.

Eyesight

Good eyesight is essential for safe driving. You should be able to read a car number plate from a distance of 20.5 metres (67 feet); for newer-type number plates the distance is 20 metres (66 feet).

When the time comes to take your test, soon after leaving the waiting room, the examiner will ask you to read a car number plate. This will be a little further away than the specified distance. If you cannot read it you will be asked to attempt it again a few steps closer. If you still have problems, the examiner will choose another number plate and use a tape measure to mark out the exact distance (this will depend on the type of number plate). If you still cannot read it, you will fail the test and will not be asked to drive.

You're allowed to wear glasses or contact lenses if necessary, but remember that if you wear glasses or contact lenses to read the number plate, you must continue to wear them the whole of the time you are being tested.

If you have any doubts about your ability to meet the eyesight requirements easily, seek advice from an optician before you start to drive.

Most people are able to detect movement to the left and right without moving their heads. This is called your 'field of vision' and is normally 180°. Some people suffer from a severely restricted field of vision, which is referred to as 'tunnel vision'. People with tunnel vision can see only a little to the left or right without moving their heads. If you suffer from this problem, you should seek advice from an optician.

If you are colour blind it does not stop you from driving, but you should make sure that your driving instructor is aware of your problem. Driving instructors will want to be extra sure that you can recognise road signs by their shapes and understand the sequence of lights at traffic signals and pelican crossings, as this is more difficult without the colour to help you.

The Theory Test

Before you can take your practical driving test you will have to take and pass the Theory Test. You should be studying for this alongside your practical driving as this allows you to relate the theory to practice on the road.

The test is in two parts: multiple-choice questions and hazard perception assessment.

In the multiple choice section you will be asked 50 questions on a touch-screen, each with a choice of answers. You need to get 43 of them correct to pass.

In the hazard perception section you will be shown 14 video clips from the driver's view. Each has at least one hazard (one has two) which develops into a situation where you might have to take action. You should click when you spot a hazard that's likely to cause you to slow down or change direction. Depending on your response you can score up to 5 marks on each clip. You will need to score 44 to pass. You will be given your result at the end of the test and you will have to pass both parts of the test at the same sitting.

More information and help can be obtained from BSM's book Theory Test for car drivers or go online to: www.bsm.co.uk.

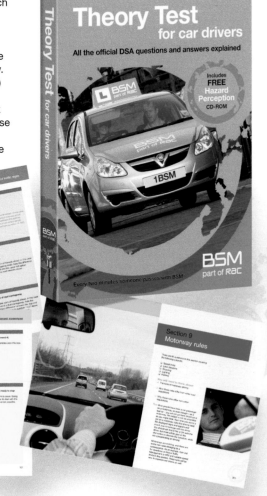

Section 2
The accompanying driver

Government statistics show that newly qualified drivers have a significantly greater chance of having a crash than more experienced drivers. This risk decreases as more miles are driven and more experience is gained.

Professional tuition with a driving instructor is a key part of the learning process required to pass the driving test and develop a higher level of skill as a newly qualified driver, but private practice is also extremely important.

When practice is carefully structured from the start, and is supervised by an experienced driver, the risk of a crash in the early months and years of driving is significantly reduced.

Three-way partnership

This book sets out a framework for a successful three-way partnership between the learner, the accompanying driver and the driving instructor. It explains the skills the learner needs to gain before they are ready to take their test and gives the accompanying driver the opportunity to help them achieve a safer driving life beyond the test.

This section describes the role taken by the accompanying driver. You could be a parent or guardian, other relative or family friend. Before both learner and accompanying driver can take to the public roads together, there are a number of things that you will need to check if you want to stay legal. Both the accompanying driver and the would-be learner are jointly responsible for ensuring that both meet the requirements.

Your licence
As the accompanying driver, you must:

❑ have held, and still hold a full EC/EEA driving licence for three years in the category of vehicle being driven

❑ be at least 21 years old

❑ not charge for driving lessons or accompanying another driver unless you are an Approved Driving Instructor (ADI). This includes accepting money for fuel.

The accompanying driver's vehicle
The car must be:

❑ taxed, and the tax disc displayed on the nearside (left) corner of the windscreen

❑ insured for use by the learner and for yourself

❑ fitted with L-plates (D-plates in Wales) of regulation size so that they can be seen

■ A valid tax disc must be displayed on the left side of the windscreen.

from both front and rear (do not put L-plates on the windscreen or rear window as they will restrict vision)

❑ in a roadworthy condition

❑ have a valid MOT certificate if the vehicle is more than three years old.

You will also need an internal mirror properly adjusted so that you have a good view to the rear.

The practical requirements
Even as an experienced driver it still takes time to get used to driving a different car to your own, as every car feels and handles differently. Bear in mind that for a learner, this lack of familiarity can be quite alarming and disorientating and it may take them some considerable time to adapt.

If your car is larger and more powerful than the one in which the learner has their driving lessons, this may cause the learner problems when judging the car's position and when carrying out manoeuvres. It can also be a

14

■ You will need your own internal mirror.

problem if the indicators, windscreen wipers or other ancillary controls are positioned in a different place. Also, if your car suffers minor defects, for example a weak parking brake or a stiff clutch pedal, the learner may struggle.

Remember to cover up or remove the L-plates when the vehicle is being used by a full-licence holder.

Ensure that you have sufficient time not only to supervise the practice sessions, but also to plan them in advance. Check the learner's Track Record and talk to their instructor about what you need to cover in each session.

Give directions clearly and with plenty of warning in order to give the learner time to respond safely. Never use a mobile phone while accompanying your learner driver.

Finally, bear in mind that these days, many tuition cars are fitted with dual controls, which makes the essential task of learning basic car control much safer than in a private vehicle.

Are you suitable?

Before you do finally decide to take on the responsibility of accompanying a learner driver, there are a number of personal factors that you may find useful to consider.

Your own driving
The learner you accompany will, in all probability, attempt to copy the way you drive. This applies both before and after passing the test. Take a look at your own driving and ensure that you still keep to the rules and follow the correct procedures.

Check the latest copy of The Highway Code. Have a chat to the instructor to discuss how things might have changed since you learned to drive. Consider having some tuition yourself, where the instructor can give you some hints and tips on sitting with a learner. Take a look at the RAC Advanced Driving Course on pages 163–165.

15

Conflicts

You may find that the driving instructor has taught the learner a different technique or procedure to the one you learned and have probably always used. Advances in technology have to some extent changed experts' views on the safest way to control a car in certain situations.

If you have any doubts or worries, feel free to discuss them with the instructor, who will be happy to explain the reasons behind any differences. You are likely to cause the learner considerable confusion if you start to argue with them or insist that they do something your way. Inevitably, the learner will try to drive exactly as their instructor has taught them.

Patience

To help the learner progress to being a safe driver most effectively, allow the instructor to focus on teaching them each aspect of the syllabus and confine your role to ensuring they have ample opportunity to practise what they have been taught. Be aware that you may find this frustrating and you will be required to exercise considerable patience.

No two people learn at the same pace; while some learners master co-ordinating the controls with ease, others may take many hours of practice. Similarly, some people have great car control but find it difficult to develop road sense and risk-perception.

■ Allow the instructor to focus on teaching the learner the syllabus.

16

Tension will nearly always slow a learner's progress, as will negative criticism that knocks their confidence. If you can make their practice sessions enjoyable, the learner is likely to progress much faster. So do try to be positive, and do not worry about how many times the learner gets the same thing wrong. Offer encouragement to try again, and praise even the smallest achievement.

You should also show patience with other road users, since they may not always allow for the fact that your car is being driven by a learner.

Ensure that you have sufficient time not only to supervise the practice sessions, but also to plan them in advance. Give route directions clearly and with plenty of warning in order to give the learner time to respond safely.

When to start

You should check with the instructor about when it is appropriate to start accompanying the learner on practice sessions. To a certain extent, this will depend on the ability of the learner, their level of confidence and your own, the type of car they will practise in, and local geography.

Both the Driving Standards Agency and BSM advise not to start practising too early. A bad experience can destroy your confidence or that of the learner. It is certainly best to wait until the learner has a reasonable ability to use the basic controls. You may easily create danger if the learner cannot move off, accelerate, brake and steer with reasonable fluency.

Where to practise

Each of the sections in this book suggests the type of road, route and traffic conditions that are likely to be appropriate. Do remember that, in the early stages of learning to drive, the learner may need you to drive them somewhere safe and suitable before you change seats and let them behind the wheel to practise.

Leaving things to the experts

Stick by the general rule that it is best to leave the driving instructor to take responsibility for all that is taught to the learner. Your task is to create safe and legal opportunities for the learner to practise what they have been taught.

For safety reasons, there are three specific skills which BSM suggests should be left entirely to the instructor:

1. Controlled stop – obviously the learner may encounter a real-life situation while practising that requires them to stop in an emergency. However, practising this on a public road can be dangerous and is best left to be taught by and practised with the professional instructor.

2. Other than in average rainy conditions you should not accompany a learner to practise in adverse weather conditions. Practising with learners in bad weather can be highly dangerous. Learners should only be accompanied by an Approved Driving Instructor in poor weather conditions.

3. Motorway driving – learner drivers are not, of course, allowed on the motorway. However, when they have passed their test, the newly qualified driver's first trip down a motorway can be quite alarming.

Using this book in conjunction with the skills to be practised

Each session focuses on one key skill and is designed to complement the learner's professional driving lessons. It follows the same set of skills as laid out in the learner's Track Record so you can keep up to date with their progress. Some practice sessions include suggestions for more advanced exercises once the learner has mastered the basic skill. All the sessions follow a similar structure and can include the following sections:

- ❏ Highway Code references

- ❏ The skill or skills to be practised

- ❏ When and where to practise

- ❏ General safety considerations

- ❏ Major points to check during practice

- ❏ Suggested advanced exercises.

At the end of each practice session it is very helpful to both the learner and their instructor if you:

- ❏ discuss how things went with the learner and see if you can both agree about what went well and what went badly

- ❏ record details of the practice session in the spaces provided at the back of this book

- ❏ make brief comments about progress or problems that you feel the instructor needs to be aware of.

■ The four standard headings address the learner, the accompanying driver, both learner and driver, and the learner with advice on what the examiner will expect.

Your instructor

Your instructor will discuss your prog. and talk you through what you need to practise throughout the lesson. Leaving s distances will be discussed while covering other key skills in your lessons. You will learn how to maintain safe distances on all t ad and issues that affect

Accompanying driver

Explain what is to be practised and t few moments to discuss what your lea has been taught by their instructor. Che out their Track Record which how they are developin

Yc

Advanced exercises

Practise:

a on all types of road

b unprompted.

Give a recap of h ise them f

Your examiner

There should always be a safe distance between yourself and other vehicles, takin into account the road and traffic conditior at the time. When you are stationary in you shoul que th

Section 3
Understanding your car

No one expects you to be a car mechanic, but you will be expected to answer questions or demonstrate how to carry out the basic maintenance of your car when you take your Practical Test.

■ Make sure your windows and windscreen are clean before every trip.

20

Maintenance checks

Making regular checks on your car can:

- keep you legal and safe

- save your fuel and is therefore eco-friendly

- prolong its life.

Daily checks
You need to know how to make daily checks before you make your journey. Walk around your car and look for obvious problems – flat tyres, damage to lights, loose trim, etc. Make sure that everything carried in the car is secure, and that the windscreen and windows are clean.

Weekly checks
The easiest way of remembering the list of checks you need to make is the acronym P-O-W-E-R:

P = Petrol (or diesel)
Make sure you have enough fuel for your journey. Allow extra in case you get caught in traffic.

O = Oil
Check the oil level and top it up if necessary. This might be from a dip stick under the bonnet, or, in the case of some modern cars, an indicator light on the dashboard. Check the brake fluid level and also the clutch fluid, which might be in a different container.

If the oil pressure or brake warning lights come on while driving, stop as soon as you can and get help. If you are changing the oil, you should dispose of the old oil to a local authority recycling point.

■ Water

W = Water

Check the radiator or expansion tank for the coolant level. Do this when the engine is cold. If hot, the scalding water could spray over you as you remove the cap. Top up the windscreen washer bottle.

E = Electrics

Make sure all the lights and indicators are working. Get someone to help you check the brake lights. Keep spare bulbs in the car, just in case. (If you travel abroad, this will be a legal requirement.) Check that all battery connections are tight and clean. You should dispose of old batteries at a local authority recycling point.

R = Rubber

Check the tyres; make sure the tread is well above the minimum legal limit and that there are no cuts or bulges in them. Check the tyre pressures when they are cold. Your car will use more fuel if your tyres are incorrectly inflated. Remember to check the spare.

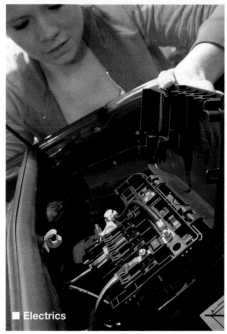

■ Electrics

■ Rubber

■ Fan belt

■ Wiper blades

You also need to check that:

☐ the fan belt is tight and not worn

☐ the wiper blades are clearing the windscreen.

Your instructor

Your instructor will explain the different parts of the engine by opening the bonnet and showing you how to carry out checks. You will be asked questions to ensure that you have remembered what you have been taught.

Accompanying driver

Make sure that your learner knows how to make these checks on the car you are using. Refer to the manufacturer's handbook and go through the checks with them.

The examiner

At the start of your Practical Test you will be asked two questions. These questions are in pre-set combinations and comprise one 'show me' question and one 'tell me' question (see pages 147–149). Failure to answer one or both of these questions correctly will result in one driving fault being recorded.

Section 4
The 45 key skills

Use this book alongside your Track Record to guide you through the requirements of each key skill.

Your instructor will discuss your progress and complete the Track Record with you. So remember to take it with you when you go for a lesson.

Each time you and your instructor cover a skill, your instructor will record the date and a number from 1 to 5 denoting the level reached in that skill.

The key for the 1 to 5 scale is:

1. Skill introduced

2. Skill carried out under full instruction

3. Skill carried out when prompted

4. Skill carried out with minimal prompts

5. Skill carried out without prompts

Your aim is to be able to carry out each skill independently without any prompting from your instructor or accompanying driver. Only then will you be ready to take your test. There are 45 driving skills, each with five assessment levels.

There is no set order and your instructor will assess when to introduce each skill. This will depend on:

❑ your progress

❑ the area where you learn

❑ the time you take your lessons (with regard to the road, traffic and weather conditions).

Once you have achieved a completed Track Record your instructor will arrange for you to have a Mock Test.

If you want to achieve that goal of passing first time, don't take your test too early.

1 The cockpit drill

HIGHWAY CODE
97, 99-100, 102

While you are learning to drive you will always be climbing into a driving seat that someone else has just been sitting in. Because we all vary so much in size and build, chances are you will need to adjust the seat and mirrors in order to be safe and comfortable.

This is the sequence of actions you should go through each time you get into the car.

It is easily remembered as DSSSM – Doors, Seat, Steering, Seat belt, Mirrors.

Doors
Make sure that all the doors are properly closed. If you are in any doubt, get out and see.

Seat
Your seat needs to be in a position so that you can reach the foot controls easily. The pedal on the left, called the clutch, goes down the furthest. Push that one to the floor and adjust the seat so that you are not stretching for it but have a slight bend in the knee when it is pressed to the floor.

Raise your foot up and down a couple of times. If your knee hits the steering wheel you can lower the seat (some cars have height adjustment) or raise the steering wheel.

Steering
You need to be able to move your hands freely around the steering wheel. Place both hands at the top of the wheel. You should have a slight bend in your elbows. If you have to stretch or are too close, you can change the angle of the back of the seat on most cars.

Next, check the head restraint. This is very important, as it will minimise the risk of whiplash in an accident if it is properly adjusted. The top of the head restraint should be roughly in line with the top of your ears. When taking the driving test the passenger seat must also have a head restraint.

Seat belt

Always wear your seat belt. This is a legal requirement. Any passengers must also belt up. If there are seat belts in the back of the car, passengers must wear them. You are legally responsible for anyone under the age of 14 and must make them wear their seat belts.

Mirrors

You should have three mirrors on your car. The interior one should be adjusted so that you can see as much of the rear windscreen, and therefore the road behind, as possible without having to move your head. The door

mirrors need to show a sliver of the car down the edge of the mirror and be angled so that you can see as far down the road as possible. They should show half road and half everything else. Adjust the mirrors while parked on a level road. When taking instruction, practising or on a test, another internal mirror must be fitted.

Once you have passed your test and own your own car, you may well be the only person who drives it. The seat, therefore, will always be in the correct position. The mirrors, though, ought to be checked every time. Someone could have knocked the door mirrors and you could have knocked the interior mirror. You may also find that you seem to settle down as the day goes on and when you get in the car in the evening your posture has changed to such an extent that the mirrors need readjusting.

Before you switch on the engine you must get into the habit of checking that the parking brake is firmly on and the gear lever is in neutral. If you leave the car in gear and do not check, your car might leap forward and stall as you start up. Make these two checks part of your routine.

Your instructor

Your instructor will show you how to make any adjustments in the car. You will be expected to do this as a matter of routine and unprompted every time you get into the car.

Accompanying driver

Make sure that your learner knows where the appropriate adjustments can be made as it is likely that they are a different size and build to you. Remember you too should do this once the session is over and before you drive the car again yourself.

Your learner also needs to know where all the ancillary controls are, and the meaning of any dashboard lights.

The examiner

Your examiner will expect you to do your cockpit checks when you get into the car. Make sure you are comfortable and can reach all the controls. Take your time and don't rush.

So:

❑ make sure that the doors are closed

❑ check that your seat belt and head restraint are properly adjusted

❑ check your mirrors to give maximum view

❑ fasten your seat belt.

Before you start the engine, make sure that the parking brake is on and the gear lever is in neutral.

If you stall at this stage, don't panic – it doesn't necessarily mean you have failed. Try to relax and restart the engine.

2 Use of car controls and instruments

HIGHWAY CODE
126, Annex 6

You do need to know enough about the controls of a car to be able to operate them properly while driving. A basic understanding of what you do to make a car move is, therefore, advisable. If you want or expect to get the best from your car, you need to use the controls sympathetically. A greater understanding will also help you drive in an ecological way and therefore become more fuel-efficient.

So let's take each control in turn and explain what you need to know about it.

Accelerator

The pedal on the right is called the accelerator. Instructors usually refer to it as the 'gas pedal', simply because it is quicker to instruct 'More gas' than it is to say, 'Press the accelerator down a little further'. It is operated by the right foot and controls the speed of the car. The further down you press it, the faster the engine runs, which in turn drives the car's wheels faster.

When you ease off the gas pedal the engine runs more slowly and the car slows down. It is a very sensitive pedal – only slight pressure is required to get a result. You need to be able to operate this control smoothly, and it is probably best to rest your heel on the floor and just use the ball of your foot and toes to work the pedal.

Foot brake

The middle pedal is the foot brake. It is also only operated with your right foot because there is usually no need to be speeding the car up while simultaneously slowing it down. The foot brake works on all four wheels of the car. Don't stamp on this pedal but squeeze it progressively until the car comes to a stop and, as it does so, ease off the pedal to avoid a jolt. When you touch the brake, two red brake lights come on at the back of the car, informing other road users that you are slowing down.

Clutch

The pedal on the left is the clutch. It is operated with the left foot and is used to move the car away, to change gear and to stop the car without stalling the engine. Imagine you are a passenger in a car and the driver stops at a red light. The engine keeps running because the driver puts the clutch down as the car comes to a stop, and in doing so disconnects the engine from the wheels. The clutch allows the wheels of the car to stop turning, without the engine cutting out.

As the driver moves away again the driver raises the clutch, enabling the engine to drive the wheels.

Gears

The gear lever is always operated together with the clutch. The gears are used to match the speed of the engine to the speed of the car. As the car picks up speed you need to select a higher gear. Each gear has a limited amount of power; the higher the gear, the less the power, but greater the speed.

Imagine having to push a car out of the way because it has run out of petrol. It is heavy, but, as soon as you have some momentum, it takes far less effort to keep it rolling. Similarly in driving, in order to get the car moving you need the gear with the most power, which is the first gear.

Once the car is moving, you can change up one or more gears once you are at the appropriate speeds. Slowing down is the same. You need to match the gear to the speed of the car, so that when you come to accelerate again the car has the right amount of power to go.

It is not always necessary to go up and down through the gears in order. It is often better to skip a gear in order to match the speed of the engine to the road speed. This means that if you are in fourth or fifth gear and need to stop at red lights, you can brake to a stop and then select first gear to go.

You need to practise moving the gear lever into the various positions, because when you are driving you should keep your eyes on the road ahead when changing gear.

Parking brake

The parking brake is used to secure the car once it has stopped. Normally, it only works on the car's back brakes. To apply it, you push the button in and pull it up. To release the parking brake, pull it up slightly and push the button in, then drop the lever to the floor.

Ancillary controls

You need to familiarise yourself with all the ancillary controls of the car. The indicators can be found on either the left or the right of the steering wheel. Know where your lights are and how to operate the windscreen wipers, de-mister and heaters.

Steering

Try not to look down at the end of the bonnet because this can affect your steering. Looking well ahead helps keep the car in a straight line. So keep your head up and your eyes high. Keep both hands on the steering wheel. Position them at ten-to-two, or a quarter-to-three. Remember, it is normally only the front wheels that steer. When you turn left, the back wheels cut in and will mount the kerb if you steer too early. When turning right, you will cut the corner if you steer too early.

■ Hands at the ten-to-two position.

Your instructor

Your instructor will take you to a safe place to explain all the controls. You will be given an opportunity to make your first attempt to move off away from other traffic. At the end of the lesson your instructor will recap on what you have covered to make sure you have understood everything and explain what the plan is for the next lesson. Your Track Record can be completed accordingly.

Accompanying driver

It is a good idea to leave the first controls lesson to the instructor and listen to the advice he or she gives you about the right time to have your first session. If you have been driving for several years, controlling a car has become second-nature and it is easy to forget how difficult it can be for some to master.

Your examiner

If it begins to rain, or if visibility is restricted for any reason, your examiner will expect you to know where to access the wipers, de-mister, lights, etc. You should know the meaning of all the displays on the instrument panel. Remember to use all the controls in an eco-friendly manner, balancing the clutch and accelerator to move away safely.

You need to:

❑ accelerate evenly

❑ avoid stalling or excessive revving of the engine

❑ choose the correct gear in good time

when dealing with hazards so that you are not steering and trying to change gear at the same time

❑ brake evenly and in good time

❑ apply the parking brake when necessary

❑ ensure that you can control the steering by good control of the steering wheel

❑ steer at the correct time and smoothly.

How the clutch works

The same principles apply in a four-wheel drive car.

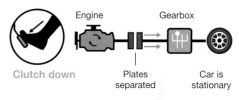

Clutch down — Plates separated — Car is stationary

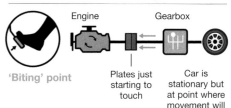

'Biting' point — Plates just starting to touch — Car is stationary but at point where movement will commence

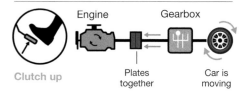

Clutch up — Plates together — Car is moving

31

3 Controlling the clutch

HIGHWAY CODE
122, 159

You need to be able to control the clutch to ensure a safe and smooth drive. The clutch is the link between the engine and the gears. When you press the clutch pedal you disconnect this link and therefore the engine runs freely without any drive.

When you move off, you need to learn to bring the clutch into play so that the engine can drive the car. This takes practice and the more you have, the better you will become at moving off, and gear changing, smoothly.

Try not to be frightened of stalling and depressing the clutch too early, or for an excessive time.

Do not keep your foot on the clutch pedal when steering around a bend or corner, as your control will be affected by having no engine drive.

Your instructor

Your instructor will discuss your progress and talk you through what you need to practise throughout the lesson. Your lesson will be planned to take into account your needs. If you need to practise finding the biting point (the point where the clutch links with the engine), this can be done either off road or on road throughout the lesson.

At the end of the lesson your instructor will recap on what you have covered to make sure you have understood everything, and explain what the plan is for the next lesson. Your Track Record can be completed accordingly.

Accompanying driver

Explain what is to be practised, discuss what the instructor has taught the learner and check the Track Record to see how they are developing this skill. There will be times when your learner wonders why they didn't learn in an automatic. Practice is the key to achieving smooth clutch control, so, if your learner is having difficulty getting it right on the road, take some practice sessions off road, until it becomes second-nature. Make sure your learner:

❑ selects the correct gear

❑ uses sufficient gas

❑ finds the clutch biting point

❑ co-ordinates the parking brake if moving off

❑ can control the clutch to creep forwards and stop.

You can practise clutch control throughout other planned lessons such as manoeuvres or emerging at junctions.

Give a recap how they have done and praise them for their efforts, even if they have found it difficult. Discuss the session with them by asking them to assess their own performance.

Your examiner

Throughout the test your examiner will expect you to demonstrate good clutch control. Smooth gear changes and good co-ordination with the accelerator and gears is required. Remember to depress the pedal just before stopping so you do not stall.

4 Moving off safely

HIGHWAY CODE
159, 161, 184, 229

Now that you know about the controls of the car, you need to know how to use them to get the car moving. For some, the biggest nightmare is stalling the first time you move away. With a good instructor you should be able to move the car smoothly, even the first time you attempt it. It is important that you are able to move away without endangering other road users.

When you are prepared and ready to move, you need to look for a safe gap. This means a gap that is big enough for you to pull into without causing any other road user to slow down, swerve or stop.

Look in your mirrors, especially the interior and right-door mirrors. If the road behind looks reasonably clear, have a look over your right shoulder into the area not covered by your mirrors – the blind spot. You are looking for vehicles, cyclists or pedestrians coming out of driveways or trying to cross the road. You also need to check the road ahead, making sure that oncoming vehicles aren't on your half of the road.

This is all part of a routine called Mirrors-Signal-Manoeuvre or MSM.

The manoeuvre part is any change of direction or change of speed. In moving off you are changing both direction and speed, so you need to use the MSM routine. Having checked your mirrors, blind spots and the road ahead, you should decide if you need to signal.

Before you move, look round for a final check to make sure that it is still safe. The situation can change very quickly, especially when you are new to it all. Don't be afraid to take your time at first. The observations are extremely important. With practice you will be able to

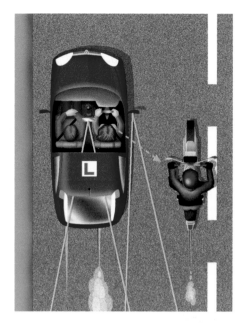

■ You won't see objects in your interior and right-door mirror blind spots, so look over your shoulder as well.

look for, and decide on, a safe gap much quicker.

Your instructor

Your instructor will discuss your progress and find an appropriate place for you to move off. This might be a quiet road at the beginning and become progressively busier as your control and observations improve.

At the end of the lesson your instructor will recap on what you have covered to make sure you have understood everything, and explain what the plan is for the next lesson. Your Track Record can be completed accordingly.

Accompanying driver

Explain what is to be practised and take a few moments to discuss what your learner has been taught by their instructor. Check out their Track Record which will show you how they are developing this skill.

For the first few practices the ideal place is an empty car park where the learner can go through the routine without endangering others. Do not attempt to practise this on a busy road before your learner is ready. Make sure you:

❏ avoid areas where children are playing

❏ always check if it is safe to move off

❏ make sure you are a reasonable distance from any car parked ahead of you; it should only be necessary to steer very slightly in order to reach the normal driving position

❏ be ready to take control of the steering when moving off and parking.

Make sure your learner:

❏ carries out the cockpit drill correctly and reasonably quickly

❏ completes the safety checks before starting the engine in the correct sequence

❏ uses the correct gear, adequate gas, clutch at biting point and parking brake

❏ considers if a signal is necessary

❏ co-ordinates the controls smoothly as the car starts to move

❏ steers adequately

❏ assumes normal driving position

❏ uses the MSM routine.

When stopping, make sure your learner:

❏ uses the MSM routine

❏ brakes gently to a stop

❏ positions reasonably close to the kerb.

They may find balancing control with safe observations difficult at first. However, the more often this is practised the easier it will become for your learner.

Advanced exercises

Practise:

a remaining on a quiet road, timing your learner's ability to move off safely; this will prepare them for busier roads

b moving off with the radio on so that your learner cannot hear the sound of the engine change at clutch biting point; this will help when other traffic noise drowns the sound of the engine

c gradually moving off in busier roads, practising selecting the first safe gap in the traffic

d moving off at traffic lights.

Give a recap how they have done and praise them for their efforts, even if they have found it difficult. Discuss the session with them by asking them to assess their own performance.

Your examiner

Your examiner will expect you to move off safely and under control.

So make sure you:

- ❑ use the MSM routine

- ❑ check your blind spots for traffic and pedestrians

- ❑ consider whether a signal is required

- ❑ make balanced use of the gas, clutch, brakes and steering

- ❑ use the appropriate gear.

■ **Check the road ahead before pulling around the parked car – a vehicle parked on the other side of the road might force an oncoming driver into your path.**

5 Moving off at an angle

HIGHWAY CODE
159

If another car is parked close to your car, you may have to move off at a sharp angle. This procedure is similar to pulling away in a straight line, but you may need to move very slowly in order to give yourself time to steer. Keep the gas at an even rate and, as you let the clutch pedal up to the biting point, the car will start to move. A slight pressure on the clutch pedal will slow you down or bring the car to a stop again.

Ease the clutch up a fraction and you will creep forwards again. Then creep forwards or backwards a few inches at a time whenever you are in a confined space or need to edge forwards to see clearly.

Use the Mirrors-Signal-Manoeuvre (MSM) routine – look in your mirrors, especially the interior and right-door mirrors. If the road behind looks reasonably clear, have a look over your right shoulder into the area not covered by your mirrors – the blind spot. You are looking for vehicles, cyclists or pedestrians coming out of driveways or trying to cross the road. You also need to check the road ahead,

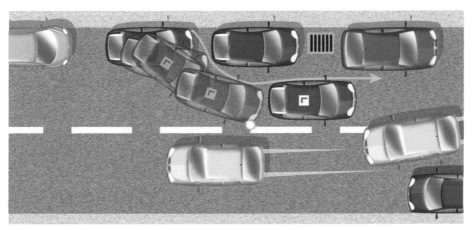

making sure that oncoming vehicles aren't on your half of the road. Keep looking all around. Decide whether you need to signal.

Before you move, have a final check all around, including blind spots, to make sure that it is still safe.

Your instructor

Your instructor will discuss your progress and find an appropriate place for you to move off at an angle. While this might be a quiet road at the beginning, the instructor will pick busier ones as your control and observations improve. You will learn how to balance your clutch control with accurate steering.

At the end of the lesson your instructor will recap on what you have covered to make sure you have understood everything, and explain what the plan is for the next lesson. Your Track Record can be completed accordingly.

Accompanying driver

Explain what is to be practised and take a few moments to discuss what your learner has been taught by their instructor. Check out their Track Record which will show you how they are developing this skill.

Practising this exercise can make the learner nervous due to the close proximity of the other parked vehicle. Before attempting this you may wish to imagine a parked car ahead and check the learner's confidence by carrying out the practice and moving out around the pretend car. Alternatively, you could position a tall cone or other marker in a quiet road to represent the offside rear of a parked car.

Before you start this session, find a quiet, level road which is reasonably wide with sufficient gaps between the parked cars to allow the learner to park about a car length behind the vehicle in front.

Make sure you:

- ❑ check their knowledge and understanding of the skill

- ❑ avoid any road where children are playing

- ❑ personally check that it is safe before moving off

- ❑ keep looking all around as the car starts to move

- ❑ look particularly for oncoming traffic into whose path the learner might pull out

- ❑ are aware that the learner may not correct the steering quickly enough and finish positioned too wide or on the wrong side of the road

- ❑ are sensitive to the drivers of parked cars – your L-plates may make them apprehensive as they see the learner get closer and closer to their car.

Make sure the learner:

- ❑ prepares the controls of the car to be ready to move – correct gear, adequate gas, clutch at biting point and parking brake

- ❑ observes to check it is safe, including blind spot check

- ❑ signals if necessary

- ❑ achieves slow speed with clutch control

- maintains smooth co-ordination as the car starts to move

- steers briskly

- corrects steering to achieve the correct driving position

- selects a safe place to stop

- uses the MSM routine when stopping

- brakes gently to a stop

- positions accurately when stopping by the kerb.

Advanced exercises

Remain on a quiet road, and gradually reduce the gap from the parked car in front.

Practise on:

a slightly busier roads, attempting to take advantage of the first safe gap in the traffic

b an uphill gradient

c a downhill gradient where brake control will be necessary.

Give a recap of how they have done and praise them for their efforts, even if they have found it difficult. Discuss the session with them by asking them to assess their own performance.

■ Take advantage of the first safe gap – but watch out for other road users, such as motorcyclists, who might be trying to overtake the slower cars.

Your examiner

Your examiner will ask you to pull up on the left just before a parked vehicle. You need to be able to show you can move off under control using the MSM routine, judging whether you need to signal, steering safely away from the parking space. Don't forget to look ahead as well as behind for traffic.

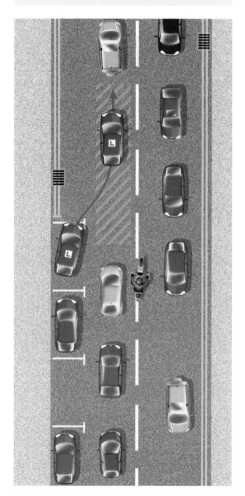

6 Moving off uphill

HIGHWAY CODE
159-161, 243, 252

You will need to use your accelerator, clutch and parking brake together to prevent your car from rolling back. So when moving away uphill you should:

- ❏ put the car in first gear

- ❏ press the accelerator pedal a bit harder than you would on the level; the engine has more work to do so it needs more power

- ❏ let the clutch out slowly to the biting point and release the hand brake

- ❏ keep the car stationary or let it move forwards slightly. Do not let it roll backwards. Do not jerk or allow the car to stall. Keep pressure on the gas pedal as you let the clutch out smoothly all the way. Do not race the engine.

If you're returning to your car after having parked on a hill, remember your front wheels should be pointing away from the kerb.

Your instructor

Your instructor will discuss your progress and find an appropriate place for you to move off uphill. This is an excellent exercise for practising your control skills – you will need to judge the balance of the accelerator, clutch and parking brake, while making all the correct observations.

Your instructor will find an appropriate place to practise. If you live in a hilly area, this exercise will become a priority, as you may have to move off uphill in every lesson.

At the end of the lesson your instructor will give a recap of what you have covered to make sure you have understood everything, and explain what the plan is for the next lesson. Your Track Record can be completed accordingly.

Accompanying driver

Explain what is to be practised and take a few moments to discuss what your learner has been taught by their instructor. Check out their Track Record which will show you how they are developing this skill.

Make sure you:

- ❏ check their knowledge and understanding of the skill

- ❏ avoid any road where children are playing

- ❏ personally check that it is safe before moving off

- ❏ do not allow the learner to over-rev the engine for any length of time.

Make sure your learner:

- ❏ carries out cockpit drill correctly

- ❏ completes safety checks before starting the engine

- ❏ selects the correct gear

- ❏ applies the foot brake firmly

- ❏ releases the parking brake

- ❏ keeps the car still while observations are carried out, such as checking the blind spot

☐ signals if necessary

☐ moves away smoothly without rolling back

☐ steers to the correct driving position

☐ uses Mirrors-Signal-Manoeuvre (MSM) routine to stop safely

☐ parks accurately and smoothly facing uphill.

Advanced exercises

Practise:

☐ on a quiet road, use a stopwatch to encourage reducing the time it takes to move away safely

☐ with the radio on so that the engine note cannot be heard

☐ on busier roads to develop judgement in selecting the first safe gap in the traffic

☐ on steeper hills

☐ at traffic lights on hills.

Give a recap of how they have done and praise them for their efforts, even if they have found it difficult. Discuss the session with them by asking them to assess their own performance.

Your examiner

If you live in a hilly area you will have to show that you can move off safely throughout your test. You will be asked at some time during your test to pull over at a convenient place on a hill.

You will be expected to move off safely and under control, using the MSM routine. You will also be expected to judge whether a signal is necessary.

7 Moving off downhill

HIGHWAY CODE
159-161, 243, 252

When moving off downhill you need to use the foot brake to control the speed and not the clutch. The control procedure is different, too. You should:

❑ engage first gear, but if the hill is very steep you may need a higher gear

❑ apply the foot brake

❑ release the parking brake

❑ release the foot brake slowly and, as the car starts to roll forward, release the clutch smoothly and use the accelerator gently.

If you are returning to your car after having parked on a hill, remember that your front wheels should be pointing towards the kerb.

Your instructor

Your instructor will discuss your progress and find an appropriate place for you to move off downhill. This is an excellent exercise for practising your control skills as you will need to judge the balance of accelerator, clutch and foot brake, while making all the correct observations.

Your instructor will find an appropriate place to practise. If you live in a hilly area this exercise will become a priority, as you may have to move off downhill in every lesson.

At the end of the lesson your instructor will recap on what you have covered to make sure you have understood everything, and explain what the plan is for the next lesson. Your Track Record can be completed accordingly.

Accompanying driver

Explain what is to be practised and take a few moments to discuss what your learner has been taught by their instructor. Check out their Track Record which will show you how they are developing this skill.

Make sure you:

❑ check their knowledge and understanding of the skill

❑ avoid any road where children are playing

❑ personally check that it is safe before moving off

❑ do not allow the learner to over-rev the engine for any length of time.

Make sure your learner:

❑ carries out cockpit drill correctly

❑ completes safety checks before starting the engine

❑ selects the correct gear

❑ uses the foot brake

❑ releases the parking brake

❑ keeps the car still while observations are carried out, including the blind spot

❑ signals if necessary

❑ moves away smoothly

❑ steers to the correct driving position

❑ uses Mirrors-Signal-Manoeuvre (MSM) routine to stop safely

❑ parks accurately and smoothly facing downhill.

Advanced exercises

Practise:

a on a quiet road; use a stopwatch to encourage reducing the time it takes to move away safely

b with the radio on so that the engine note cannot be heard

c on busier roads to develop judgement in selecting the first safe gap in the traffic

d on steeper hills

e at traffic lights on hills.

Give a recap of how they have done and praise them for their efforts, even if they have found it difficult. Discuss the session with them by asking them to assess their own performance.

Your examiner

If you live in a hilly area you will have to show that you can move off safely throughout your test. You will be asked at some time during your test to pull over at a convenient place on a hill. You will be expected to move off safely and under control, using the MSM routine. You will also be expected to judge whether a signal is necessary.

8 Changing gear

HIGHWAY CODE
122

Your instructor will talk you through this in the early stages. When changing gear you need to:

❏ check your mirrors

❏ cover the clutch

❏ move your hand to the gear lever

❏ press the clutch down, off gas

❏ select the required gear

❏ bring the clutch up slowly with a little gas

❏ check your mirrors and, if safe, give a little more gas.

As you develop, you will use your own skill and judgement of when and where to change gear. You do not need to change up or down progressively through each gear but 'block' change such as fourth to second and third to fifth.

Your instructor

Your instructor will discuss your progress with you and explain what the lesson will include. At first your instructor will find a safe place and talk you through the gear-changing exercises. You will be taught how to 'palm' the gear lever correctly and practise a smooth gear change. Your instructor will prompt you to change gear at the appropriate time for the manoeuvre you are about to make, using all the correct routines.

It will also be explained that careful use of accelerator, brake and gear-changing can save fuel and therefore be eco-friendly.

As you progress through the five stages of your Track Record, your instructor will prompt you less and less.

At the end of the lesson your instructor will recap on what you have covered to make sure you have understood everything, and explain what the plan is for the next lesson. Your Track Record can be completed accordingly.

Accompanying driver

Explain what is to be practised and take a few moments to discuss what your learner has been taught by their instructor. Check out their Track Record which will show you how they are developing this skill.

For the first few practices you need a long, quiet straight road. To start with, tell your learner when to change gear, so think well ahead and give the instruction in good time. Make sure you:

❏ avoid any road where children are playing

❏ personally check that it is safe before moving off

❏ are a reasonable distance from any car parked ahead of you

❏ tell the learner when to change gear (to start with)

❏ do not ask the learner to change gear when too close to a parked car.

Make sure your learner:

❑ uses the mirrors effectively

❑ places hand on gear lever appropriately without looking down

❑ completes the gear change before the car slows down too much

❑ stays in control of the steering

❑ pushes the clutch right down and comes off the gas at the same time

❑ selects the appropriate gear

❑ lets the clutch back up with a little gas

❑ returns both hands to the steering wheel.

Advanced exercises

As your learner develops you can allow them to make their own judgements about the gear they need to select. If they need prompting, then do so. Practise:

a on uphill and downhill gradients

b using the block-changing method making sure your learner is travelling at the correct speed for the gear they are about to engage

c slowing to a stop in the high gears and engaging first gear while the car is moving slowly.

Give a recap of how they have done and praise them for their efforts, even if they have found it difficult. Discuss the session with them by asking them to assess their own performance.

Your examiner

Your examiner will observe you throughout the test and check that you are in the appropriate gear for the speed and any manoeuvre you need to take. You will be expected to use your own judgement and skill; there will be no one to prompt you.

Try not to:

❑ look down at the gears while changing

❑ select the wrong gear for the traffic conditions

❑ travel any amount of time with the clutch pedal depressed (coasting).

9 Steering

You need to steer your car both in a steady course and varying degrees of angles so you can deal with hazards and junctions.

Hold your hands in the ten-to-two or quarter-to-three position. Feed the rim of the steering wheel through your hands in the direction you wish to go. You might find it useful for your instructor to demonstrate this method.

Steering accurately is linking the amount of lock required with balancing the speed on approach. Going too fast will cause erratic steering.

You will also need to be able to take one hand off the steering wheel to change gear, or use the auxiliary controls, without swerving.

Your instructor

Your instructor will discuss your progress and find an appropriate place for you to practise and demonstrate the 'pull-push' method to you if required.

At the end of the lesson your instructor will recap on what you have covered to make sure you have understood everything, and explain what the plan is for the next lesson. Your Track Record can be completed accordingly.

Accompanying driver

Explain what is to be practised and take a few moments to discuss what your learner

has been taught by their instructor. Check out their Track Record which will show you how they are developing this skill.

There are two steering exercises to practise: steering in a straight line and steering to turn a corner or manoeuvre. Steering in a straight line or to keep a normal driving position on the road normally only requires very slight movements of the steering wheel.

This can initially be practised on a quiet, reasonably straight road or a car park.

Make sure you:

❑ are able to use the 'pull-push' method of steering yourself before embarking on this session

❑ are ready to take control of the steering wheel should the need arise

❑ prompt them the moment you feel they are leaving things too late

❑ only practise 'pull-push' steering at slow speeds, with little or no gas, or using clutch control to keep the car slow.

Having turned the steering wheel in one direction, learners often forget that they need to turn the wheel back in the opposite direction in order to straighten up.

Make sure your learner:

❑ moves off safely

❑ steers in a straight line with both hands on the wheel

❑ remains in a straight line when changing gear

❑ turns the wheel back after steering at the correct time

❑ does not let the steering wheel spin back.

Make sure your learner avoids:

❑ steering when stationary, as this can damage the tyres

❑ crossing their hands on the steering wheel

❑ letting the steering wheel spin back.

Give a recap of how they have done and praise them for their efforts, even if they have found it difficult. Discuss the session with them by asking them to assess their own performance.

Advanced exercises

If you live near a suitable off-road centre you may be able to practise steering through slaloms. Alternatively you could book a lesson on a BSM driving simulator if one is conveniently nearby.

Your examiner

You will need to show that you can steer safely and appropriately throughout the test. You need to steer accurately and smoothly, balancing it with the other controls such as gear-changing and acceleration.

Losing control of the steering, such as mounting a kerb or continually battling with the steering wheel, means you are not ready for your test.

10 Stopping normally

HIGHWAY CODE
238-252

When stopping you will be changing your speed and direction. You should therefore use the Mirrors-Signal-Manoeuvre (MSM) routine.

You should also use **PSL**:

P   position the car correctly for any change in direction you need to make

S   speed – adjust your speed appropriately

L   look for any other road users or danger.

Look for a safe and legal place to stop that's not going to inconvenience other road users. Always know what is going on behind you while you are looking. When you see a place to stop, ensure you have enough time to:

❑ check your mirror and decide if you need to signal

❑ take your foot off the accelerator

❑ apply the brake, lightly first then more firmly

❑ press down the clutch pedal just before you come to a stop

❑ make sure you are in a safe position and apply the parking brake

❑ put the gear lever into neutral

❑ if you are stopping for any length of time, switch off your engine and avoid static running, which wastes fuel and unnecessarily adds to pollution.

Try not to stop too close to the vehicle in front as this could cause you problems when moving off again.

Your instructor

Your instructor will discuss your progress and find an appropriate place for you to practise. You will be given advice on where it is safe to stop and the routine that's needed to undertake the manoeuvre safely.

At the end of the lesson your instructor will recap on what you have covered to make sure you have understood everything and explain what the plan is for the next lesson. Your Track Record can be completed accordingly.

Accompanying driver

Explain what is to be practised and take a few moments to discuss what your learner has been taught by their instructor. Check out their Track Record which will show you how they are developing this skill.

In the early stages you can begin by suggesting places for your learner to stop.

Make sure you:

❑ give them enough time to understand your instruction and think about what they are going to do – so plan well ahead

❑ check their routine as they slow down and stop at junctions or traffic lights.

Make sure your learner:

❑ uses the MSPSL routine (see section 15)

As your learner gains experience you can ask them to find a safe and convenient place to park. This will test their own judgement of safety and control.

Give a recap of how they have done and praise them for their efforts, even if they have found it difficult. Discuss the session with them by asking them to assess their own performance.

Your examiner

You will be expected to choose a safe, legal and convenient place to stop, close to the edge of the kerb, where the vehicle will not obstruct the road and create a hazard. You need to stop under control using all the correct safety routines.

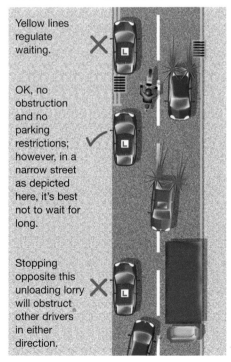

Yellow lines regulate waiting.

OK, no obstruction and no parking restrictions; however, in a narrow street as depicted here, it's best not to wait for long.

Stopping opposite this unloading lorry will obstruct other drivers in either direction.

■ Stop safely in a place where you are allowed to wait. Don't stop opposite a vehicle stationary on the other side of the road if it would cause an obstruction.

11 Controlled (emergency) stop

HIGHWAY CODE
118, 120, 122

Having learned to stop normally, you need to learn the skill of stopping in an emergency. Your main aim should be to stop promptly in the shortest possible distance without losing control of the car. This means moving your foot off the gas pedal and onto the brake as quickly as possible.

It needs to become a reflex rather than something you consciously think about. This is because what is happening in front of you at this time is far more important.

Grip the wheel firmly with both hands. This helps you to keep the car under control and also acts as a brace, preventing you from being thrown forwards as you stop.

Anti-lock braking system (ABS)

Most modern cars are fitted with an anti-lock braking system. This activates when the brakes are applied harshly, as in an emergency. It automatically and very quickly releases and reapplies the brakes as it senses the wheels are about to lock. The sensation of this can be heard and felt through the brake pedal, and when this happens you should keep your foot hard down. Although an anti-lock system will not shorten your stopping distance, it will allow you to steer.

Power-assisted steering requires the engine running in order to work properly, so it is important that the car does not stall, risking the loss of steering control. Make sure you:

❑ apply maximum pressure on the brake pedal and keep it there until the car comes to a stop

❑ disengage the clutch by pressing the clutch pedal, to prevent the engine stalling

❏ steer around the hazard if necessary.

When you have stopped, make the car safe by applying the parking brake and selecting neutral. You are likely to be stopped in the middle of your side of the road. Check mirrors and both blind spots before pulling away.

If you stamp on the foot brake too fiercely in a vehicle without an anti-lock braking system you risk locking the wheels of the car and causing a skid. Prevention is better than cure, so always try to brake progressively and firmly in the first place. Should you, however, lock the wheels, you will recognise this from the screeching noise the tyres make on the road surface. Make sure you:

❏ release the brake immediately and then reapply it as soon as the wheels have started turning again.

If you skid:

❏ steer into the direction of any skid; if the back end is moving to the right, steer right to bring it back in line

❏ try not to panic; take your foot off the brake as quickly as possible.

Your instructor

Your instructor will talk you through this exercise and find a quiet and safe spot to practise. Your instructor will ensure that there is no following traffic when practising.

All new cars have had anti-lock brakes fitted following a European Union mandate that came into force in July 2004. Because your practice car – or the car you may buy when you pass your test – may not be so new, it may not have ABS fitted, so your instructor will explain the procedure for both stopping

in a car fitted with ABS and a car without ABS fitted.

If necessary, your instructor will be able to demonstrate this exercise for you in our car which will be fitted with ABS.

Accompanying driver

It is advisable that this exercise is left to the instructor. However, you can discuss the theory of the skill in case an incident does occur.

Check your car's handbook for advice on braking and to find out if ABS or a stability system is fitted. Keep in mind that ABS is one of the car's primary safety features. It cannot, however, cross the boundaries of physics – if this safety feature is fitted, don't let it tempt the learner into taking risks when driving. Road safety can only be achieved by adopting a responsible driving style.

Your examiner

You might have to do this as an exercise during your test. Your examiner will check all around before asking you to stop. You will be expected to bring the car to a stop under full control, without locking the wheels, in good time. Don't forget to make effective observation when moving off again.

12 Using the mirrors effectively

HIGHWAY CODE
97, 133, 161, 163, 179-180, 182, 184,
202, 229, 234-235, 267, 288-289

You need to know as much about what is happening on the road behind you as you do about what is taking place in front. This is because the situation behind can change very quickly; and that means you must look in your mirrors frequently and always be aware of what may be in your blind spots.

But just looking is not enough; you must also act sensibly and safely based on what you see. Make sure all your mirrors are adjusted correctly as part of your cockpit drill and that you are using them to their full advantage.

You must always use your mirrors before doing anything which might affect other road users, such as:

❏ signalling

❏ changing direction

❏ turning left or right

❏ overtaking or changing lanes

❏ stopping or slowing down

❏ increasing speed

❏ opening your car door.

Using your mirrors well is the key to making you a safe driver. You need to be constantly updating yourself on what is all around your car, so that nothing comes as a surprise to you. When approaching any hazard you need to know what is behind you as it could affect the way you deal with the situation.

Watch out for cars and pedestrians close by when you park. Look before you open your car doors and wait, if necessary.

Your instructor

Your instructor will discuss the importance of using the mirrors, not only as part of the Mirrors-Signal-Manoeuvre (MSM) routine, but as constant information about what is happening all around.

At the end of each lesson your instructor will recap on what you have covered to make

49

sure you have understood everything, and explain what the plan is for the next lesson. Your Track Record can be completed accordingly.

Accompanying driver

Explain what is to be practised and take a few moments to discuss what your learner has been taught by their instructor. Check out their Track Record which will show you how they are developing this skill.

This key skill will continue throughout your learner's progress. It is important that the learner not only looks in the mirrors and takes in the information, but that they then act safely on what they see. If they make a mistake, it's a good idea to pull up and stop and use a question-and-answer session.

You can include this key skill within other sessions. Make sure you:

- check their knowledge and understanding of the skill

- personally check the mirrors before giving directions

- watch their eyes for mirror checks

- prompt the MSM routine if necessary.

Make sure your learner:

- uses the MSM routine where necessary

- acts safely on what they see in the mirror

- uses the left-hand mirror just before turning left, after a controlled stop and after moving off after being stationary at junctions.

Advanced exercises

Practise:

a at busier times of the day

b at complex junctions

c in rural (country) areas

d without prompting.

Give a recap of how they have done and praise them for their efforts, even if they have found it difficult. Discuss the session with them by asking them to assess their own performance.

Your examiner

Your examiner will watch your eyes and can tell if you are checking the mirrors. There is no need to move your head, or try to make it obvious. You should show full and effective use of all mirrors throughout the test. The mirrors must be checked carefully before signalling, changing direction or changing speed, and the MSM routine should be displayed.

13 Giving signals

HIGHWAY CODE
103-112, page 104

Signals are the language of driving. They warn other road users that you are there, or that you intend to change speed or direction in some way.

Always use your mirrors as part of the Mirrors-Signal-Manoeuvre (MSM) routine. Make sure you:

❑ only use the signals shown in The Highway Code

❑ give them early and clearly so others can see and respond to them

■ **Giving arm signals to other road users:**

I intend to move in to the left or turn left

I intend to move out to the right or turn right

I intend to slow down or stop

❑ they are not misleading or confusing

❑ consider when and if a signal is required.

Signalling does not give you the right to any priority and you should never signal without checking your mirrors.

Make sure that you time your signal correctly; start your MSM routine with enough time so that your signal is not late.

Ensure that your signals are not misleading. For example, imagine giving a signal to pass a parked car where there is a junction on the right. A driver waiting to emerge from the right may see the signal and suppose that you are turning right. The driver may also presume that you will be slowing down to make the turn and that there will be enough time to slip out.

Put yourself in the other driver's place.

Arm signals

For most occasions, as when changing direction, an indicator is better than an arm signal because it:

❑ can be seen more easily, especially at night

❑ can be given for longer

❑ allows you to keep both hands on the steering wheel.

Ensure you know and can give the arm signals shown in the Highway Code as they can be useful to use at low speeds in traffic and when slowing on the approach to a pedestrian crossing. You also need to understand their meaning if any other driver uses them.

Never wave pedestrians across the road. You could put them in danger from another vehicle.

Other signals

Early and progressive braking gives following drivers the time to see your brake lights and warns them that you are slowing down.

The horn is also a signal, but it should only be used to warn of your presence, never used as a rebuke. Never use it when you are close to animals.

Reversing lights show that either you or another driver intends to back up, perhaps into a parking space.

■ **Brake light and reversing light signals**

I am applying   I intend to reverse
the brakes

Your instructor

Your instructor will discuss the importance of giving correct signals in good time. You will also be encouraged to make a decision about whether a signal is necessary at all, and not just signal without thinking about it first.

At the end of every lesson your instructor will recap on what you have covered to make sure you have understood everything, and explain what the plan is for the next lesson. Your Track Record can be completed accordingly.

Accompanying driver

Explain what is to be practised and take a few moments to discuss what your learner has been taught by their instructor. Check out their Track Record which will show you how they are developing this skill. Practising this key skill should continue throughout all your learner's sessions. Remember that their performance can rise and fall as they learn other key skills.

Make sure you:

❑ check their knowledge and understanding of the skill

❑ give directions in good time.

Make sure your learner:

❑ considers whether a signal is necessary

❑ avoids misleading signals

❑ understands the meaning of the signals given by others.

Advanced exercises

Practise:

a at busier times of the day

b at complex junctions

c without prompting.

Give a recap of how they have done and praise them for their efforts, even if they have found it difficult. Discuss the session with them by asking them to assess their own performance.

14 Acting on signs and signals

Your examiner

You are expected to give signals clearly to let other road users know your intended course. Only signals shown in The Highway Code should be used, including to pedestrians.

Signals should be given in good time and cancelled after the manoeuvre has been completed. You must not ever beckon pedestrians to cross the road.

14 Acting on signs and signals

HIGHWAY CODE
104-112

You need look out for signs and signals as you drive. You need to know what they mean, and act on them promptly and safely.

Traffic signs giving you an order are normally circular. Triangular signs give warnings and rectangular signs give directions or information.

Road markings may be used for any of the above.

Traffic lights change in a set cycle and are designed to control the traffic at junctions. You need to know their meaning and act correctly on what you see.

■ **Traffic light signals**

RED means 'stop' and wait behind the stop line on the road.

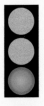

GREEN means you may go on if the way is clear.

RED AND AMBER also means 'stop'. Don't pass through or start to move until GREEN shows.

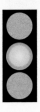

AMBER means 'stop' at the stop line. You may go on only if you have already crossed the stop line when AMBER shows or are so close to it that to pull up might cause an accident.

There are certain people who, when give a signal to stop, you must obey.

These are:

❏ police officers

❏ traffic officers

❏ traffic wardens

❏ school crossing patrollers

❏ Vehicle & Operator Services Agency (VOSA) officers (in England and Wales)

❏ Highways Agency (HA) officers ('A' class roads and motorways in England and Wales).

You must also look out for the signals given by other road users. Such as:

❏ indicators

❏ hand signals

❏ brake lights

❏ reversing lights.

Treat flashed headlights as a warning, not an invitation to proceed with priority. If they are flashed as an invitation, it is your decision whether to accept.

Knowing your traffic signs is not just about passing the Theory Test, you must be able to put the theory into practice on the road.

■ **Police signals: Stop**

Traffic approaching from the front

Traffic approaching from both front and behind

Traffic approaching from behind

■ **Police signals: Beckon traffic on**

From the side

From the front

From the front*

* In Wales signs appear in English and Welsh on clothing and vehicles of emergency services.

■ Arm signals to persons controlling traffic

I want to go straight on

I want to turn left (use either hand)

I want to turn right

■ Motorcyclist indicator signals

I intend to move out or turn to the left or the right

I am applying the brakes

■ Motorcyclist arm signals

I intend to move out or turn to the left or the right

I intend to slow down or come to a stop

Your instructor

After discussing your progress, the instructor will talk you through what you need to practise throughout the lesson. At first your instructor will prompt you, but gradually you will find yourself in busier areas where you will use your own judgement to deal with situations safely. You may be asked what traffic sign you have just passed, so make sure you look out for them.

After the lesson your instructor will recap on what you have covered to make sure you have understood everything, and explain what the plan is for the next lesson. Your Track Record can be completed accordingly.

Accompanying driver

At the start, your learner will be concentrating on the control of the vehicle and might find it difficult to follow road signs or road markings. You will need to prompt them at first, then gradually introduce them to busier roads with less prompting, as their standard improves.

Make sure you:

❏ check their knowledge and understanding of the skill

❏ personally check it is safe each time your learner changes speed or direction

❏ give directions in good time so the learner can follow road and direction signs correctly.

Make sure your learner:

❏ understands the meaning of signs and signals

❏ acts correctly and safely on all signs and signals.

Practise:

❏ on busier roads and complex junctions

❏ allowing your learner to follow a set route unprompted, following all the direction signs.

Give a recap of how they have done and praise them for their efforts, even if they have found it difficult. Discuss the session with them by asking them to assess their own performance.

Your examiner

You need to show that you understand and are able to respond to all traffic signs and road markings. Act correctly at traffic lights – when the green light shows, check that the road is clear before proceeding. All signals given by police officers, traffic wardens, school crossing patrols, VOSA Officers or HA Traffic Officers must be obeyed.

You should have the awareness to be able to respond to signals given by other road users, and be ready to act correctly.

15 Turning left

HIGHWAY CODE
182-183

You need to know how to turn safely from the road you are on into a side road.

Remember the Mirrors-Signal-Position-Speed-Look (MSPSL) routine.

Identify the road into which you wish to turn by looking for clues. There may be advanced warning with a sign or you might be able to see traffic emerging or turning into the road. You can look for gaps in the buildings or between parked cars.

Once you have located the junction, and while you are assessing it, you need to start putting the MSPSL routine into practice. Imagine that you are going to make a left turn from a major road into a minor road.

VOSA (Vehicle and Operator Services Agency) provides a range of licensing, testing and enforcement services with the aim of improving the roadworthiness standards of vehicles.

HA (Highways Agency) Traffic Officers work to keep traffic moving and ensure safety, dealing with everything from First Aid to traffic management.

Mirrors
Check behind in your mirrors to see the position of any following cars, motorcyclists or pedal cyclists. At this stage, you are looking to see if it is going to be safe to give your signal.

Signal
Give this in good time.

Position
Remain in your normal driving position, about a metre from the kerb. The position of your car acts as a signal and confirms to other road users that you do not in fact intend parking on the left before the junction. Try to maintain this position throughout the turn.

Speed
This needs to be at its lowest just before the turn, with the correct gear selected. In order to do this you need to start slowing the car down with the foot brake early. The less you can see into the new road, the slower you need to go. If there are any problems around the corner, such as parked cars or children playing in the road, you will then be able to stop the car safely.

Often second gear will match the speed at which you need to take the turn. Select second gear approximately two car lengths from the turn because this will give you plenty of time to raise the clutch. Maintain this speed with either the gas on a level road or travelling uphill, or the foot brake if you are travelling downhill.

Look
Check your mirrors again, especially the left-door one. Check the road ahead to see if anyone is waiting to turn right into the same road. Check into the new road for any problems you may need to deal with, and also because this will help you to determine when to start steering. Once you have turned into the new road, check behind. If safe, gently accelerate.

Your instructor

Your instructor will discuss your progress and talk you through what you need to practise throughout the lesson. The left turn is the easier of the junction manoeuvres as you do not have to cross the path of road users coming the other way. Your instructor will talk you through at first but gradually allow you to make your own judgement on using the MSPSL routine, control of your car including your approach speed, and the safe completion of the manoeuvre.

At the end of the lesson your instructor will recap on what you have covered to make sure you have understood everything, and explain what the plan is for the next lesson. Your Track Record can be completed accordingly.

Accompanying driver

Explain what is to be practised and take a few moments to discuss what your learner has been taught by their instructor. Check out their Track Record which will show you how they are developing this skill.

It is recommended that you do not attempt this practice session until the learner has been taught by their instructor both to turn left from major to minor roads and also to emerge left from minor to major roads.

If possible, you need to choose a quiet series of level roads with good visibility where you can keep going around the block, turning and emerging to the left. If you start on a major road your first left turn will be into a minor road. The next time you turn left it will probably be into a major road. From the major road you can turn left again into a

■ Your position one metre from the kerb signals to other road users that you are intending to turn into another road and not park before the junction.

minor road and so forth until you are back where you started.

Make sure you:

☐ avoid junctions where cars are parked too close to where you wish to turn, before or after the turn

☐ are prepared to prompt and/or take control if necessary

☐ check that all manoeuvres are safe

☐ if approaching too fast, prompt your learner in good time.

Make sure that your learner:

☐ uses the mirrors effectively

☐ gives correct signals at an appropriate time

☐ takes up the correct position before turning

☐ drives at an appropriate speed on approach

☐ observes before turning

☐ steers sufficiently and at correct time to turn

☐ does not swing out before or after turning

☐ straightens wheel at the correct time

☐ checks the mirrors after turning into the new road

☐ corrects the steering in good time

☐ gives the correct signals.

Advanced exercises

Practise:

a on hills facing up and down

b where cars are parked near the junction

c where there are pedestrians and other traffic

d at traffic lights

e in a higher gear and change down as appropriate.

Give a recap of how they have done and praise them for their efforts, even if they have found it difficult. Discuss the session with them by asking them to assess their own performance.

Your examiner

You will be expected to approach the junction safely using the MSPSL routine, judging your speed and engaging the appropriate gear. You should show the ability to judge the correct speed of approach and take up the correct position.

When turning left, the vehicle should be over to the left to avoid swinging out. Watch out for cyclists and motorcyclists coming up on your left and pedestrians who are crossing.

Effective observation must be given before moving into a junction and making sure it is safe before proceeding.

16 Emerging left

HIGHWAY CODE
170-178

As you approach the end of a road, start assessing it and noticing the road markings, if there are any. Try to decide whether you could class the junction as 'open' or 'closed'.

Open – **you have a good view into both sides of the new road:**

If you have a unrestricted view into the new road and you can see that it's clear of any other traffic – and provided there isn't a Stop sign across the road you're on – you can make the decision to emerge far sooner than if the view into the new road were restricted. Your emerging speed will then be dictated by how much control you need to steer into the new road safely and smoothly.

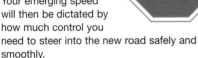

Closed – **you can see very little of the new road into which you wish to emerge:**

If your view into the new road is virtually nil, you need to be prepared to slow down and even stop in order to look and emerge safely into a gap.

Whatever the visibility on the approach, you still need to make full use of the Mirrors-Signal-Position-Speed-Look (MSPSL) routine.

Start the routine early to give yourself plenty of time to slow the car down and assess the junction. Once you reach a point from where you can see into the new road, start looking for a safe gap in the traffic. It is important that you take a good look in both directions.

For a left turn you need to know whether there are any obstructions or whether any traffic is overtaking and on your half of the road.

You need to look right again to check that what you saw the first time has not changed. The situation can change very rapidly and if it was safe to emerge the first time you looked, you simply need to be certain that this is still the case.

If you can't see, edge forwards. Keep your head moving all the time. You need to check that, when you emerge, you don't cause any other driver to slow down, swerve or stop. This may mean that you need to pick your speed up rapidly to merge safely with the rest of the traffic.

Your instructor

Your instructor will discuss your progress and talk you through what you need to practise throughout the lesson. You will be given the opportunity to practise many different types of junction, depending on your ability at the time.

Gradually you will find yourself in busier areas where you will use your own judgement to deal with the junction safely.

At the end of the lesson your instructor will recap on what you have covered to make sure you have understood everything, and explain what the plan is for the next lesson. Your Track Record can be completed accordingly.

Accompanying driver

Explain what is to be practised and take a few moments to discuss what your learner has been taught by their instructor. Check out their Track Record which will show you how they are developing this skill.

Check that they understand the different road priorities and the meaning of Give Way and Stop signs and road markings.

If possible, you need to choose a quiet series of level roads with good visibility where you can keep going around the block, emerging and turning left, just as in the previous session.

It is recommended that you do not attempt this exercise until the learner has been taught by their instructor both to turn left from major to minor roads but also to emerge left from minor to major roads.

Make sure you:

❑ check their knowledge and understanding of the skill

❑ avoid practising where cars are parked too close to the junction where you wish to turn, whether before or after the turn

❑ personally check it is safe each time before you turn right

❑ are especially aware that the learner may find it difficult to judge the speed of other traffic and select a safe gap

❑ are ready to prompt the learner to steer or, when absolutely necessary, to take control of the wheel yourself

❑ prompt the learner to slow down in good time if the speed is too fast on approach.

When the learner first practises this exercise, it's safest for them to be in second gear on approach. To begin with, the learner is likely to stop and select first gear before emerging,

but will gradually learn to slow down and give way as appropriate.

Make sure your learner:

❑ understands the Mirrors-Signal-Position-Speed-Look (MSPSL) sequence and how to use it

❑ uses mirrors effectively

❑ gives correct signal at an appropriate time

❑ takes up correct position on approach

❑ adjusts speed appropriately on approach

❑ observes before/during emerging

❑ selects a safe gap

❑ steers sufficiently and at correct time to turn

❑ positions correctly in the major road

❑ checks the mirrors after turning into the new road

❑ accelerates sufficiently on the major road to avoid causing other vehicles to slow down.

Advanced exercises

Practise:

a on hills facing up and down

b where there are parked cars near the junction

c where there are pedestrians and other traffic

d at closed junctions where you will need to stop

e where visibility is very restricted and you need to edge forwards to see better

f at open junctions where you may be able to slow down and emerge without stopping

g all the above but approach in third or a higher gear and change down as appropriate.

Give a recap of how the learner has done and praise them for their efforts, even if they have found it difficult. Discuss the session with them by asking them to assess their own performance.

Your examiner

You will be expected to approach the junction at the correct speed while using the MSPSL safety routine. You will experience several junctions on your test, and you will be expected to approach them judging the speed of approach to the layout and zones of vision.

17 Turning right

HIGHWAY CODE
170-178

When turning right into a side road use the MSPSL routine.

Mirrors
Especially the right-door mirror. Look in particular for motorbikes or cars that might be about to overtake.

Signal
Give this in good time.

Position
Steer the car over to the right slightly and position it so that it is as close to the left of the centre of the road as it is safe to be. Again, your position confirms to other road users what your signal is indicating – that you intend to turn right. If there are obstructions on the right-hand side of the road, you may need to delay your positioning.

Speed
If the road ahead is clear, your speed will be similar to the left turn. You need to be slowing down early so that you can look and assess how safe it is to make the turn.

Look
You now have to cross the path of oncoming traffic. You have two options: to go or to stop.

Go!
If the road ahead is obviously clear, check behind to make sure there is nothing about to overtake, and then look into the new road. You

are looking for any parked cars or pedestrians crossing the road. Look especially for motorbikes or cars that might be about to overtake. If there are, don't start the turn.

You are also looking to identify the point at which you need to start turning the wheel. You should turn into the road and finish in the normal driving position – about a metre from the kerb – without cutting the corner or clipping the kerb.

Stop!

If there is traffic coming towards you – or if you are in any doubt as to how safe it would be to make the turn – then don't make it. Wait and try to judge a safe gap so that you can turn without causing any other road user to slow down, swerve or stop. If you think you would have enough time to walk across the road, this is the same amount of time you would need to drive across the road.

If you practise this a few times it eventually becomes a split-second judgement where you decide, 'yes, I could walk across the road, so therefore I will drive across'; or, 'no, there wouldn't be enough time to walk safely across the road, so I will wait.'

Your instructor

There will come a time when your instructor decides continually turning to the left is enough and you can venture further into new territory by turning right. The instructor will discuss your progress and talk you through what you need to practise throughout the lesson. Listen carefully – there is a lot to think about. This is the trickier of the two turns as you have to cross the path of oncoming traffic and be aware overtaking traffic, especially motorcyclists.

At the end of the lesson your instructor will recap on what you have covered to make sure you have understood everything and explain what the plan is for the next lesson. Your Track Record can be completed accordingly.

Accompanying driver

Explain what is to be practised and take a few moments to discuss what your learner has been taught by their instructor. Check out their Track Record which will show you how they are developing this skill.

It is recommended that you do not attempt this exercise until it has been covered by the instructor. You need to choose a quiet set of level roads with good visibility where you can keep going round the block turning right and emerging to the right.

Make sure you:

❑ check their knowledge and understanding of the skill

❑ personally check it is safe each time before you turn right

❑ are especially aware that the learner may find it difficult to judge the speed of oncoming traffic and select a safe gap

❑ are always ready to prompt the learner to steer or, when absolutely necessary, to take control of the wheel yourself.

Make sure your learner:

❑ uses the mirrors effectively

❑ gives correct signal at an appropriate time

- ❑ takes up correct position on approach

- ❑ drives at an appropriate speed on approach

- ❑ selects the correct gear

- ❑ observes adequately on approach

- ❑ times approach to select a safe gap or give way as necessary

- ❑ takes up correct position before turning

- ❑ makes a final check of right-hand mirror

- ❑ steers sufficiently and at correct time to turn

- ❑ positions correctly in the minor road

- ❑ checks the mirrors after turning into the new road.

Advanced exercises

Practise:

a on hills facing up and down

b where there are no central road markings

c where there are pedestrians and busy traffic

d where there are queues of traffic

e at traffic lights

f all the above, but approach in third or a higher gear and change down as appropriate.

Give a recap of how they have done and praise them for their efforts, even if they have found it difficult. Discuss the session with them by asking them to assess their own performance.

Your examiner

You should show the ability to judge the correct speed of approach and take up the correct position. When turning right, the car should be positioned as close to the centre line of the road as it is safe to do, and when it's safe to make the turn, you should not cut the corner. Effective observation must be given before moving into a junction and making sure it is safe before proceeding.

18 Emerging right

HIGHWAY CODE
170-178

As you approach the end of a road, start assessing it and noticing any road markings. What is your zone of vision? Try to decide whether you could class the junction as 'open' or 'closed'.

Open – you have a good view into both sides of the new road:

If you have a unrestricted view into the new road and you can see that it's clear of any other traffic – and provided there isn't a Stop sign across the road you're on – you can make the decision to emerge far sooner than if the view into the new road were restricted. Your emerging speed will then be dictated by how much control you need to steer into the new road safely and smoothly.

Closed – you can see very little of the new road into which you wish to emerge:

If your view into the new road is virtually nil, you need to be prepared to slow down and even stop in order to look and emerge safely into a gap.

■ Because this major road is on a bend, your vision is restricted to both the left and right – a 'closed' junction. That's why there is a Stop sign and a solid white line on the road surface.

Whatever the visibility on the approach, you still need to make full use of the Mirrors-Signal-Position-Speed-Look (MSPSL) routine. Start the sequence early to give yourself plenty of time to slow the car down and assess the junction.

Once you reach a point from where you can see into the new road, start looking for a safe gap. It is important that you take a good look in both directions. You need to look right again to check that what you saw the first time hasn't changed. The situation can change very rapidly, and if it was safe to emerge the first time you looked, you simply need to be certain that this is still the case.

If you can't see, edge forwards. Keep your head moving all the time. In looking, you are also checking that once you do emerge, you can do so without causing any other driver to slow down, swerve or stop. This may mean that you need to pick your speed up rapidly to merge safely with the rest of the traffic.

Your instructor

Your instructor will discuss your progress and talk you through what you need to practise throughout the lesson. You will be given the opportunity to practise many different types of junction, depending on your ability at the time.

Gradually you will find yourself in busier areas where you will use your own judgement to deal with the junction safely.

At the end of the lesson your instructor will recap on what you have covered to make sure you have understood everything, and explain what the plan is for the next lesson. Your Track Record can be completed accordingly.

Accompanying driver

Explain what is to be practised and take a few moments to discuss what your learner has been taught by their instructor. Check out their Track Record which will show you how they are developing this skill.

If possible, you need to choose a quiet series of level roads with good visibility where you can keep going around the block, emerging and turning right, just as in the previous session.

It is recommended that you do not attempt this exercise until the learner has been taught by their instructor both to turn right from major to minor roads and also to emerge right from minor to major roads.

Make sure you:

❑ check that the learner understands the different road priorities and the meaning of Give Way and Stop signs and road markings

❑ avoid practising where cars are parked too close to the junction where you wish to turn, whether before or after the turn

❑ personally check it is safe each time before you emerge

❑ are especially aware that the learner may find it difficult to judge the speed of other traffic and select a safe gap

❑ are ready to prompt the learner to steer or, when absolutely necessary, to take control of the wheel yourself

❑ prompt the learner to slow down in good time, if the speed is too fast on approach.

When the learner first practises this exercise it is safest for them to be in second gear on approach. To begin with, the learner is likely to stop and select first gear before emerging, but will gradually learn to slow down and give way as appropriate. Make sure your learner:

❑ understands the MSPSL sequence and how to use it

❑ uses the mirrors effectively

❑ gives correct signals at an appropriate time

❑ takes up correct position on approach

❑ adjusts speed appropriately on approach

❑ observes before/during emerging

❑ selects a safe gap

❑ steers sufficiently and at correct time to turn

❑ positions correctly in the major road

❑ checks the mirrors after turning into the new road

❑ accelerates sufficiently on the major road to avoid causing other vehicles to slow down.

Advanced exercises

Practise:

a on hills facing up and down

b where there are parked cars near the junction

c where there are pedestrians and other traffic

d at closed junctions where you will need to stop

e where visibility is very restricted and you need to edge forwards to see better

f at open junctions where you may be able to slow down and emerge without stopping

g all the above but approach in third or a higher gear and change down as appropriate.

Give a recap of how they have done and praise them for their efforts, even if they have found it difficult. Discuss the session with them by asking them to assess their own performance.

Your examiner

You will be expected to approach the junction at the correct speed whilst using the MSPSL safety routine. You will experience several junctions on your test, and you will be expected to approach them using the correct position and speed of approach according to the layout and the zone of vision. You should find a safe gap to emerge into and avoid hesitating.

19 Approaching crossroads

HIGHWAY CODE
146, 170-178

Crossroads are places of high risk because there are many points from which another vehicle can suddenly emerge. Therefore they need to be treated with caution.

There are two main types – marked and unmarked.

Marked crossroads

If you are approaching on the main priority road with the intention of travelling straight ahead you need to recognise that you are approaching a crossroads, and you do this by looking for clues in the same way as you would do if you were approaching any other junction. This time, however, you need to identify two roads opposite each other.

Check for the position of any following vehicles and consider any signal you might need to give. If you are planning to travel straight ahead you do not need to indicate, so your signal might be the brake lights to warn other vehicles that you are slowing down.

Match your speed to what you can see. Keep braking until you can see that it is safe to proceed. It becomes safe to go on when you can clearly see the ends of the roads you are about to pass. If there are vehicles waiting to emerge, make sure they have seen you and are not going to pull out in front of you.

Where the traffic lights have turned to green – and you have moved forward to take up a position to turn right – once there's a gap in the oncoming traffic you may find there is a vehicle opposite also wishing to turn right. There are two ways of doing this – offside-to-offside and nearside-to-nearside – both of which are acceptable.

Offside-to-offside

Drive slowly, moving forwards in a straight line so that you pass the other driver on your offside, or driver's side. Stop when you are almost opposite your point of turn. This is safest because from this position you have a clear view of the road ahead.

Nearside-to-nearside

Drive slowly forwards and start to steer to the right slightly so that you pass the other driver on your nearside, or passenger's side. Again, stop when you are almost opposite your point of turn. From this position your view of the oncoming traffic may be obscured by the vehicle opposite you, so take care to make sure it is safe to complete the turn.

Your decision as to whether to turn offside-to-offside or nearside-to-nearside will depend on the following three things:

The layout of the junction

❑ If the crossroads is square, or your exit is further away from you than the opposite exit, you will find turning offside-to-offside to be the most convenient.

The road markings

❑ Arrows and boxes painted on the road showing where you should position your vehicle.

The other driver

❑ Try to establish eye contact with the other driver. If, as they start to edge forwards, they keep the wheels of the car straight you will be turning offside-to-offside. If they turn the wheels to the right, you will probably be turning nearside-to-nearside. Follow suit, if it is safe to do so. If they

appear to be doing the same as you, and waiting for your lead, position the car as you feel safest, taking into consideration the layout of the junction and any road markings.

When approaching a crossroads with a Give Way line across your road, consider the road opposite. Where there is a vehicle waiting to emerge from the road opposite, you need to strike a balance between making progress and being courteous. Try to make eye contact with the driver of the vehicle opposite, and be prepared to give way if it looks like they are about to move. There is no priority, since you are both emerging from a minor onto a major road.

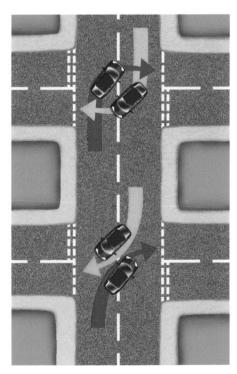

■ Offside-to-offside passing (top) and nearside-to-nearside (bottom).

Unmarked crossroads

Unmarked crossroads need to be treated with extreme caution. Another driver who is approaching the crossroads from your right or your left may assume that they have priority over you and keep travelling straight through the junction. Your speed will therefore depend on what you can or cannot see. You will need to imagine a Give Way line and to approach the junction as if you were emerging.

Your instructor

Your instructor will discuss your progress and talk you through what you need to practise throughout the lesson. You will be given the opportunity to practise many different types of junction, including crossroads, depending on your ability at the time. Gradually you will find yourself in busier areas where you will use your own judgement to deal with the junction safely.

Your instructor will give you advice about where turning nearside-to-nearside or offside-to-offside is advisable and the reasons behind the choice. At the end of the lesson your instructor will recap on what you have covered to make sure you have understood everything, and explain what the plan is for the next lesson. Your Track Record can be completed accordingly.

Accompanying driver

Explain what is to be practised and take a few moments to discuss what your learner has been taught by their instructor. Check out their Track Record which will show you how they are developing this skill.

Make sure you:

☐ check their knowledge and understanding of the skill

☐ choose a quiet time of the day

☐ know the junction layout and the normal positioning before taking your learner to practise.

Make sure your learner:

☐ approaches the junction in the correct lane

☐ uses the Mirrors-Signal-Position-Speed-Look (MSPSL) routine effectively

☐ understands the options of turning offside-to-offside or nearside-to-nearside

☐ is aware that their observation can be affected if turning nearside-to-nearside by the turning car

☐ is aware of the approaching cars in the road they have to cross.

Advanced exercises

Practise:

a at busier times

b where there are two lanes of approaching traffic at traffic lights

c unprompted.

Give a recap of how they have done and praise them for their efforts, even if they have found it difficult. Discuss the session with them by asking them to assess their own performance.

Your examiner

You need to show your ability to deal with all types of junction. You will need to select the correct speed and position on approach using the MSPSL routine. You should give way to the oncoming traffic and proceed when safe without hesitation. The turn should be made without cutting the corner (when turning right) or clipping the kerb (when turning left).

20 Roundabouts

HIGHWAY CODE
184-190

Roundabouts are designed to help keep everyone moving by mixing together several streams of traffic. Give way to traffic on the roundabout approaching from your immediate right. Do not stop if it is safe to keep moving. Use your door mirrors as appropriate; signal and position correctly for the exit you wish to take.

On approach

Look well ahead and you will have seen the warning/direction sign in good time. You need to decide the direction you are going to take and use the Mirrors-Signal-Position-Speed-Look (MSPSL) routine as necessary. Check the road markings to ensure you choose the correct lane for the exit you need to take. Give way to road users on the roundabout.

Unless the signs or road markings indicate otherwise, when taking the first exit to the left you should:

❏ choose the correct lane

❏ signal left on the approach

❏ keep to the left of the roundabout and continue signalling left to leave. Give a quick check of the nearside (passenger) mirror before you leave the roundabout.

Unless the signs or road markings indicate otherwise, when taking the exit to the right or going full circle you should:

❏ choose the correct lane

❏ signal right on approach

❏ keep to the right on the roundabout until

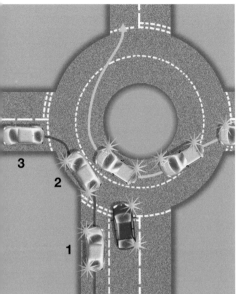

◀ Turn left: (1) left-hand lane approach, signal left, (2) keep left, and be aware of any vehicles beside you in the right-hand lane, (3) take first (left) exit onto new direction.

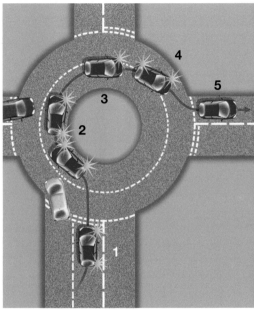

▲ Turn right: (1) right-hand lane approach, signal right, (2) keep right, still signalling right and be aware of any vehicles beside you in the left-hand lane, (3) cancel right signal and signal left after passing second exit, (4) move to left lane, (5) exit left onto new direction.

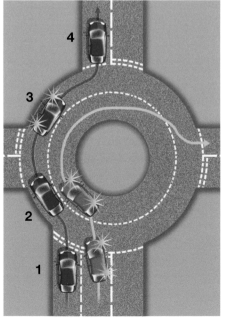

◀ Go ahead: (1) left-hand lane approach without a signal, (2) keep left and be aware of any vehicles beside you in the right-hand lane, (3) signal left after passing first exit, (4) exit left onto the road ahead.

you need to move over to take the exit (or follow any road markings)

❑ make good use of your nearside door mirror and signal left after you have passed the exit before the one you want to take.

Unless the signs or road markings indicate otherwise, when taking an intermediate exit you should:

❑ choose the correct lane

❑ not normally signal on approach

❑ stay in this lane until you need to move over to take the exit (or follow any road markings)

❑ make good use of your nearside door mirror and signal left after you have passed the exit before the one you want to take.

Your instructor

Your instructor will discuss your progress and talk you through what you need to practise throughout the lesson. You will be given the opportunity to learn about the different types, including mini-roundabouts (indicated by this sign), multiple roundabouts and more complex traffic systems. You will learn the correct way to use them under control and safely with awareness of other road users.

At the end of the lesson your instructor will recap on what you have covered to make sure you have understood everything, and explain what the plan is for the next lesson. Your Track Record can be completed accordingly.

Accompanying driver

Explain what is to be practised and take a few moments to discuss what your learner has been taught by their instructor. Check out their Track Record which will show you how they are developing this skill.

In order to practise this session efficiently it is best to try to find two or more roundabouts that are reasonably close together. You can then plan a series of routes that allow the learner to approach from different directions and exit to the left, right and straight ahead.

You can also go all the way around the roundabout, double back on yourself and approach the previous roundabout from the opposite direction. Ideally, the roundabouts should have four entrances and exits, and two or more lanes approaching and leaving.

Make sure you:

❑ check their knowledge and understanding of the skill

❑ personally check it is safe each time the learner joins a roundabout

❑ prompt the learner to slow down before it is too late if the speed is too fast on approach.

Make sure your learner:

❑ uses the MSPSL routine correctly on approach

❑ anticipates a safe gap and adjusts speed to keep moving when possible

❑ gives way when necessary

- selects the correct lane for the exit being taken

- avoids stopping at a roundabout when the vehicle behind expects them to keep moving; keep a close look behind

- avoids looking right, seeing a gap, and going without looking ahead; the car in front may not have moved, so beware.

- small roundabouts with only one lane at each entrance and exit

- mini-roundabouts.

Give a recap of how they have done and praise them for their efforts, even if they have found it difficult. Discuss the session with them by asking them to assess their own performance.

Advanced exercises

Practise on:

a busy roundabouts

b roundabouts with more than four exits

c roundabouts where the normal give way rules are changed by the road markings

d very large roundabouts which are one-way gyratory traffic systems and have many lanes, direction arrows on the lanes, and many different direction signs and exits

Your examiner

Using the MSPSL routine, show you are able to judge the correct speed of approach so that you can enter a roundabout safely or stop if necessary. You need to be positioned correctly, using the correct lane.

You should follow all direction signs and road markings looking out for all other road users, including cyclists and motorcyclists.

Effective observation should be taken throughout.

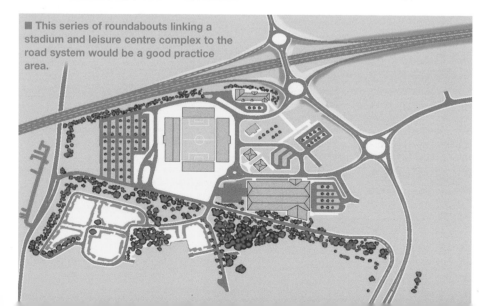

■ This series of roundabouts linking a stadium and leisure centre complex to the road system would be a good practice area.

21 Complex junctions

HIGHWAY CODE
170-178

As traffic and congestion increases, new engineering initiatives strive to solve traffic flow. Some of these junctions can be quite complicated and you need to use all your observation skills to follow direction and road signs, check road markings and avoid other road users.

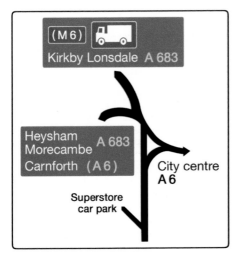

■ Sign indicating a typical, moderately complex junction ahead.

Some junctions are easier once you obtain local knowledge, but once you have passed your test your licence will allow you to drive in unfamiliar places. So you should ensure that you have all the skills to negotiate these safely while using the Mirrors-Signal-Position-Speed-Look (MSPSL) routine.

Your instructor

Your instructor will discuss your progress and introduce these more complex junctions at the appropriate time. You will cover road planning, positioning, signalling, making progress and the awareness of the other road users.

At the end of the lesson your instructor will recap on what you have covered to make sure you have understood everything and explain what the plan is for the next lesson. Your Track Record can be completed accordingly.

Accompanying driver

Explain what is to be practised and take a few moments to discuss what your learner has been taught by their instructor. Check out their Track Record which will show you how they are developing this skill.

As your learner's skill improves you can introduce them to more complex junctions. The basic rules of junctions still apply but there will be other issues to concern your learner such as direction signs and road markings. There could be lane changes to be made on approach, or an emerge onto a road with fast-moving traffic. Make sure you:

❑ check their knowledge and understanding of the skill

❑ check that they understand the different road priorities and the meaning of Give Way and Stop signs and road markings

❑ avoid practising where cars are parked too close to the junction where you wish to turn, whether before or after the turn

- personally check it is safe each time before you emerge

- are especially aware that the learner may find it difficult to judge the speed of other traffic and select a safe gap

- are ready to prompt the learner to steer or, when absolutely necessary, to take control of the wheel yourself

- prompt the learner to slow down in good time if the speed is too fast on approach.

Make sure your learner:

- plans the approach

- understands the MSPSL sequence and how to use it

- uses the mirrors effectively

- gives correct signals at an appropriate time

- takes up correct position on approach

- adjusts speed appropriately on approach

- observes before/during emerging

- selects a safe gap

- steers sufficiently and at correct time to turn

- positions correctly

- checks the mirrors after turning into the new road

- accelerates sufficiently on the new road to avoid causing other vehicles to slow down.

Advanced exercises

Practise:

a at busy times

b at night

c unprompted.

Give a recap of how they have done and praise them for their efforts, even if they have found it difficult. Discuss the session with them by asking them to assess their own performance.

Your examiner

You should show the ability to judge the correct speed of approach and take up the correct position. When turning right, the car should be positioned as close to the centre line of the road as it is safe to do, and when it's safe to make the turn, you should not cut the corner. Effective observation must be given before moving into a junction and making sure it is safe before proceeding.

When turning left, the vehicle should be over to the left to avoid swinging out. Watch out for cyclists and motorcyclists coming up on your left and pedestrians who are crossing. Effective observation must be given before moving into a junction and making sure it is safe before proceeding.

22 Pedestrian crossings

HIGHWAY CODE
191-199, 240

Pedestrian crossings are provided to help people cross the road safely. With few exceptions, even the most experienced driver is still sometimes a pedestrian. So it makes sense to ask yourself what you expect drivers to do when you wish to use a crossing. You would expect them to show consideration and to slow down or stop to let you cross.

Before you take your driving test, you may find it useful to act out the part of a pedestrian. Find a busy crossing and directions. Notice the drivers who seem to slow down and stop with ease, those who see you and are too late, and those who seem not to notice you at all. Then, when you drive again, consider the advice that follows.

There are several types of pedestrian crossings of two different kinds, controlled and uncontrolled.

Controlled crossings

Pelican
This stands for Pedestrian Light Controlled crossing. Pedestrians push a button to change the signals. When the lights are red, a steady green figure signal appears telling them they may cross.

On your approach you will see traffic lights and zigzag lines. The sequence of lights differs from that of lights controlling traffic at a junction, in that it includes a flashing amber instead of red and amber together. When the amber light is flashing you must give way to any pedestrians still on the crossing, but you can drive on if the crossing is clear.

At some Pelican crossings the lights change almost immediately as a pedestrian pushes

the button. So, once again, don't look just at the lights – look for pedestrians who might be about to push the button.

Toucan
This stands for Touch Controlled crossing. Toucans have the dual purpose of stopping the traffic for both pedestrians and cyclists. Pedestrians operate them in the same way as a Pelican crossing.

On approach you will see traffic lights and zigzag lines, but the sequence of lights is the same as at a set of traffic lights. Wherever you notice cycle routes, you should be prepared to see a Toucan crossing.

Puffin
This stands for Pedestrian User Friendly Intelligent crossing. Pedestrians push a button to change the signal. You will see traffic lights and zigzag lines on the approach. Puffins operate with an infra-red scan that holds the lights on red for as long as there is somebody on the crossing. As with the Toucan, there is no flashing amber light.

Puffin crossings are of considerable benefit to drivers because they reduce unnecessary

■ At a Puffin crossing the red and green figures are above the controller.

hold-ups in the flow of traffic. When pedestrians have crossed safely, the sequence is electronically cancelled and the light stays on green.

Equestrian crossings

These are designed specially for horse riders and work in a similar way to Toucan and Puffin crossings. They have barriers and a higher set of controls for the rider.

School-crossing patrol

The 'lollipop person' is a familiar sight to most of us. A hand-held sign on a pole stating 'Stop Children' tells drivers that they must stop. You will often see an earlier sign, 'School Patrol', which warns you that there is a school-crossing patrol ahead operating at certain times of the day. Amber lights may also flash with this sign when children are being supervised as they cross the road.

Uncontrolled crossings

Zebra crossings

You need to be able to identify that there is a crossing ahead. You do this by looking for clues. There might be an advanced warning sign, usually if the crossing is coming up around a bend or over the brow of a hill. If you are in a pedestrian area, such as near shops, you should be checking for crossings anyway.

Look for the flashing yellow beacons, zigzag lines and black-and-white stripes of the crossing itself. Try to spot them as early as possible. As soon as you have identified that you are approaching a crossing, you need to decide whether or not it is a hazard. You need to consider whether you can see:

❑ pedestrians on or around the crossing

❑ both sides clearly or whether the crossing has an obstruction.

A parked car or lorry, pedestrians, a tree, or a queue of oncoming traffic may obscure your view. You may not be able to see both sides of the crossing until you are nearly on top of it. If you can't see, you have no way of knowing if anyone is about to cross.

■ The road markings for a zebra crossing.

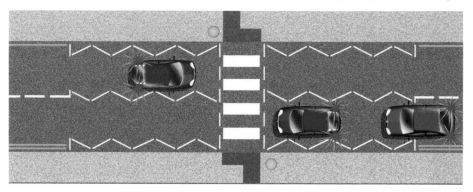

Use the Mirrors-Signal-Manoeuvre (MSM) routine. Check in your mirrors the position and speed of any following vehicles and decide whether or not you need to give a signal. The signal will usually be your brake lights, and the earlier you start to brake gently, the more warning you give to the drivers behind you.

In this situation a slowing-down arm signal can be particularly useful, especially if you are  the leading vehicle approaching the crossing. This signal does three things. It warns traffic behind and oncoming traffic of your intention to slow down or stop. It also lets the pedestrians – who cannot see your brake lights – realise that you are giving way so they are more likely to cross sooner and with more confidence, thus reducing your delay to a minimum.

If you spot pedestrians crossing early enough, you can reduce your speed sufficiently to make sure that they have finished crossing before you get there. It's the people walking along the pavement near to the crossing who can catch you out. Perhaps they will cross, or push the button at a Pelican.

Unless you have reduced speed a little, you may be too late to stop or have to brake harshly. So, anticipate the possibility, adjust your speed as needed, and be ready.

Your instructor

Your instructor will discuss your progress and talk you through what you need to practise throughout the lesson. You will be given the opportunity to experience the approach to pedestrian crossings. Your instructor will discuss with you the importance of looking well ahead and the awareness of hazards, and how you should approach crossings and how to deal with them safely.

At the end of the lesson your instructor will recap on what you have covered to make sure you have understood everything, and explain what the plan is for the next lesson. Your Track Record can be completed accordingly.

Accompanying driver

Explain what is to be practised and take a few moments to discuss what your learner has been taught by their instructor. Check out their Track Record which will show you how they are developing this skill.

Try to introduce this at a quiet time of day. By their very nature, pedestrian crossings are put where there are many pedestrians wishing to cross. It could be that they are only busy during school times, so at first introduce the crossing when they are quiet.

Make sure you:

❑ check their knowledge and understanding of the skill

❑ are aware of what is behind you when approaching a crossing

❑ look out for potential changes in the

situation, such as approaching pedestrians.

Make sure your learner:

- [ ] looks well ahead and prepares for a change in situation

- [ ] is aware of any following traffic

- [ ] stops if the lights are red

- [ ] gives way to pedestrians if the lights are flashing amber

- [ ] on an uncontrolled crossing, gives way to pedestrians waiting to cross

- [ ] waits for the crossing to clear before moving off

- [ ] does not wave anyone across.

Advanced exercises

Practise:

a at busier times of the day

b on staggered crossings

c unprompted.

Give a recap of how they have done and praise them for their efforts, even if they have found it difficult. Discuss the session with them by asking them to assess their own performance.

Your examiner

Your examiner will expect you to recognise different types of crossing and show courtesy and consideration towards pedestrians. At all crossings you should slow down and stop if there is anyone on the crossing.

At Zebra crossings, slow down and stop if there is anyone waiting. You should demonstrate your knowledge of the flashing amber light, and at all times use the appropriate routine when slowing down, stopping or moving off.

23 Level crossings

HIGHWAY CODE
167, 243, 291-299

There are several types of level crossing and you need to know how to deal with them safely.

■ Sign for level crossing without barrier or gate ahead (left) and the alternative sign for a level crossing without barrier ahead and Give Way warning.

■ Light signals ahead at level crossing (left) and the sign for a level crossing with barrier or gate ahead.

Crossings with automatic barriers

These show a steady amber light followed by twin flashing red lights when a train is approaching. You must stop. If you are on the crossing when the amber light shows, then you must keep going. Some crossings have automatic barriers, but no lights.

Open crossings

These have red flashing lights but no barriers. Where there are no lights or barriers, there will be a Give Way sign.

In rural areas there are crossings which have gates but no signal at all. Use these with extra caution; look both ways and listen. Open both gates before crossing. If you break down you must get everyone out of the vehicle. If there is time, move the vehicle. Use the railway phone if there is one. If the amber light starts to flash get well clear of the crossing.

Your instructor

You may not live in an area that has level crossings but your instructor will ensure you experience one, if possible. A short question-and-answer session will ensure you have the knowledge and understanding of the dangers at level crossings.

■ Signs for a level crossing ahead with warning lights but no gate or barrier.

Accompanying driver

Explain what is to be practised and take a few moments to discuss what your learner has been taught by their instructor. If there is a level crossing within reach of your practice session you should allow your learner to experience it, preferably when a train is due so that they can experience the lights and barriers in action. Make sure you:

❏ check their knowledge and understanding of the skill

❏ know the emergency measures in the case of an emergency.

Make sure your learner:

❏ approaches the crossing with caution

❏ obeys the signs and signals

❏ understands the different types of crossing.

Give a recap of how they have done and praise them for their efforts, even if they have found it difficult. Discuss the session with them by asking them to assess their own performance.

Your examiner

Your examiner will expect you to act on the signs and signal correctly – stopping when appropriate and waiting patiently.

24 Keeping space either side

Trying to keep space on today's roads is no easy task. As you drive, you need to achieve two aims that appear contradictory. You need to keep pace with traffic while keeping space from traffic.

Space around your car gives you time to look, think, spot risks and respond. It also provides an escape route should anything go wrong, or should anyone else make a mistake. The smaller the space around you, the greater the risk. Think that less space should equal less speed.

Look well ahead and see where your space will be reduced, and to others invading your space. Ease off the gas so you keep space in front – you will then have time to deal with problems should they occur.

When you are driving, there are only three options available: you can change speed, you can change direction or you can give a warning signal. Having enough space gives you the chance to keep all your options open for as long as possible.

Creating space and time is linked with planning and awareness skills. Looking well ahead and planning for any potential hazard will allow you the time to create space around your car.

Your instructor

Your instructor will discuss your progress and talk you through what you need to practise throughout the lesson. Improved planning and awareness skills will help you understand how leaving space can give you the time to deal with any potential problems or emergencies.

At the end of each lesson your instructor will recap on what you have covered to make sure you have understood everything, and explain what the plan is for the next lesson. Your Track Record can be completed accordingly.

Accompanying driver

Explain what is to be practised and take a few moments to discuss what your learner has been taught by their instructor. Check out their Track Record which will show you how they are developing this skill.

Creating time and space around the car can allow your learner to deal with situations without having to react late or rush routines and procedures. As their planning and awareness skills improve, their ability to create this space will improve also.

Make sure you:

❑ check their knowledge and understanding of the skill

❑ are personally aware of what is going on all around

❑ watch your learner to check that routines are well timed and not rushed

❑ balance the traffic situation with the ability of your learner.

Make sure your learner:

❑ is aware of what is all around and the importance of keeping the correct space around the car

❑ uses the Mirrors-Signal-Position-Speed-Look (MSPSL) routine if they have to

change speed and direction without having to rush

❑ eases off the gas to adjust speed accordingly

❑ has the control and awareness skills to deal with situations and controls their speed – neither too fast nor too hesitant.

Advanced exercises

Practise:

a at busier times of the day

b on more complex traffic systems

c unprompted.

Give a recap of how they have done and praise them for their efforts, even if they have found it difficult. Discuss the session with them by asking them to assess their own performance.

Your examiner

You need to show that you understand how to deal with all situations as they occur. Leaving yourself space will allow you to deal with them in good time, without being rushed or having to brake harshly.

25 Following traffic

HIGHWAY CODE
126-151, 227, 230, 235, 260, 289

Always leave enough space between you and the vehicle in front of you, so that you can pull up safely if it suddenly slows down or stops. At every speed, the safest gap to leave is your overall stopping distance.

This is the distance your car will cover before it comes to a standstill, including the time it takes you to react and the time it takes you to brake. It is the minimum distance, in good conditions, you would need if you had to use extreme braking to prevent yourself from hitting a brick wall.

Generally, at speeds over 40mph, if you leave a gap of one metre for every mph of speed, you will be able to stop safely if the vehicle in front of you pulls up suddenly. This distance is extremely difficult to judge. You might find it easier to translate distance into time by using the 'two-second rule' (this operates on the

basis that a two-second time gap gives you a distance gap of one metre per mph of your speed).

It works like this – as the vehicle in front of you passes a stationary object, such as a lamp post or a tree, you count two seconds by saying either 'only a fool breaks the two-second rule' or by counting 'a thousand and one, a thousand and two.' If you pass the lamp post or tree before you have finished counting, you are too close to the vehicle in front.

Never get any closer than your thinking distance, but be aware, your thinking distance can vary with your attention at the time. When it has been raining, or the surface of the road is greasy, you need to increase the gap. Your stopping distances virtually double, so you would be safest to double the size of the gap. Your view of the road ahead is seriously reduced the closer you get to the vehicle in front. This is especially true if that vehicle is a bus or a lorry. If you hang back you vastly

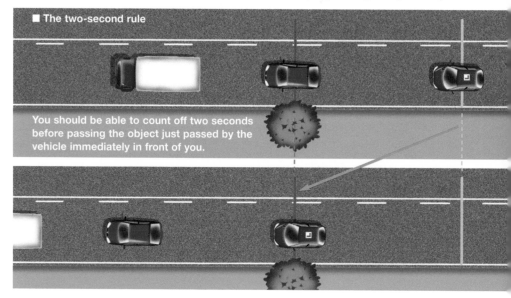

■ The two-second rule

You should be able to count off two seconds before passing the object just passed by the vehicle immediately in front of you.

increase what you can see, and therefore improve your chances of responding if they brake suddenly. You will also ensure that the driver can see you in the mirrors.

Judging a safe gap takes time and experience. If someone overtakes you and moves back in closely, check your mirrors and hang back, readjusting the gap to one that is safe between you and the new vehicle in front.

Your instructor

Your instructor will discuss your progress and talk you through what you need to practise throughout the lesson. Leaving safe distances will be discussed while covering other key skills in your lessons. You will learn how to maintain safe distances on all types of road and the issues that affect them, such as weather and heavy traffic.

At the end of each lesson your instructor will recap on what you have covered to make sure that you have understood everything, and explain what the plan is for the next lesson. Your Track Record can be completed accordingly.

Accompanying driver

Explain what is to be practised and take a few moments to discuss what your learner has been taught by their instructor. Check out their Track Record which will show you how they are developing this skill.

You can practise this on all types of road and in different weather and traffic conditions. You can include this skill while covering other ones. Make sure you:

☐ check their knowledge and understanding of the skill, including the two-second rule

☐ are aware of the effect that different road and traffic conditions have on the distances

☐ are aware of how attention can affect the thinking distance

☐ prompt your learner if they get too close.

Make sure your learner:

☐ leaves enough space to stop safely

☐ allows enough room to ensure they have a good view of the road ahead, especially when following large vehicles

☐ has an understanding of how attention can affect thinking distances.

Advanced exercises

Practise:

a on all types of road

b unprompted.

Give a recap of how they have done and praise them for their efforts, even if they have found it difficult. Discuss the session with them by asking them to assess their own performance.

Your examiner

There should always be a safe distance between yourself and other vehicles, taking into account the road and traffic conditions at the time. When you are stationary in traffic queues, you should leave space to pull out if the vehicle in front has problems.

■ A typical example of keeping space. On a two-way road you are driving in the red car at a safe distance behind the lorry.

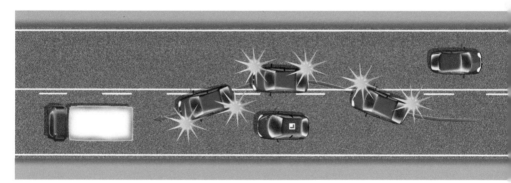

■ After the green car going in the other direction has passed, the blue car behind decides to overtake you, effectively 'stealing' your space after pulling back in.

■ It may be irritating, but it's your responsibility – after checking in the mirror that it's safe to do so – to brake gently and drop back behind the blue car to re-create your safe space.

26 Keeping pace with traffic

You need to be aware that being too hesitant or driving too slowly can be just as dangerous as driving too fast.

Drivers can become frustrated if they feel the person in front is driving too slowly for the conditions. This can lead to incidents such as a dangerous overtake, or following too closely. So as you gain confidence you need to keep up with other traffic and not allow yourself to become an obstruction on the road.

You should also avoid hesitating at junctions. Good forward planning will allow you to look and assess the situation and allow you to approach at the correct speed. You may not need to stop at all, having given yourself enough time to take good observation before turning. Try to avoid unnecessary braking.

A common occurrence at the entrance to roundabouts is hitting the driver in front. This occurs when the driver behind is looking right for a gap in the traffic. Seeing a gap large enough for both cars, the driver does not look forward again and emerges. The car in front either does not move off or hesitates, resulting in a collision.

Your instructor

Your instructor will discuss your progress and talk you through what you need to practise throughout the lesson. You will hesitate less once you have gained confidence and your control skills when moving off have become second nature. Your instructor will encourage you to make progress without making you drive too fast for the conditions or your capabilities.

At the end of each lesson your instructor will recap on what you have covered to make sure you have understood everything, and explain what the plan is for the next lesson. Your Track Record can be completed accordingly.

Accompanying driver

Explain what is to be practised and take a few moments to discuss what your learner has been taught by their instructor. Check out their Track Record which will show you how they are developing this skill.

Hesitation results from lack of confidence, judgement and control. Their ability to keep up with traffic will improve with experience and practise. Make sure you:

- ❑ check their knowledge and understanding of the skill

- ❑ are personally aware of all speed limits and conditions that affect appropriate speed

- ❑ do not show frustration if your learner is holding up traffic

- ❑ encourage and prompt your learner if they are having difficulty with control or judgement at junctions.

Make sure your learner:

- ❑ is aware of what is going on behind

- ❑ does not take your encouragement as a chance to take a risk or break the speed limit

- ❑ does not drive at a speed beyond their ability to deal with hazards or changing situations.

Advanced exercises

Practise:

a on higher-speed roads such as dual carriageways

b at busier junctions and roundabouts

c at junctions with a good zone of vision on approach so they can emerge safely without stopping.

Give a recap of how they have done and praise them for their efforts, even if they have found it difficult. Discuss the session with them by asking them to assess their own performance.

Your examiner

You need to show your ability to drive at a realistic speed for the road and traffic conditions. All hazards should be approached at a safe, controlled speed, without being overcautious or interfering with the progress of other traffic.

27 Meeting traffic

HIGHWAY CODE
155

Where the road narrows to less than the width of two vehicles and there is a vehicle approaching from the opposite direction, you might both want to use the same space. This is called a 'meet situation'.

Check behind to see the position and speed of any following vehicles. While you are slowing down, you need to assess the actions of the approaching driver. Slowing down early will allow more time to decide what to do next.

If an approaching driver is slowing down, resulting in both of you reaching the gap at the same time, you will need to be looking for a safe place to stop. This will allow the other driver to come through the gap first.

If there are parked cars on either side you need to be looking for gap to pull into or opposite to allow the other driver through. If you pull into a gap, leave yourself plenty of room to pull away again. Check behind and consider a signal before doing so.

The Highway Code says that where the obstruction is on your side of the road you

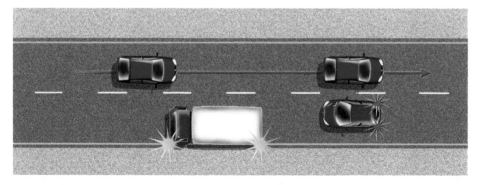

■ A lorry has parked on the left to unload, creating an obstruction. Because the obstruction is on the same side of the road as the red car, its driver should give priority to the blue car.

87

should give way to any approaching traffic. Where, however, the obstruction is on the opposite side of the road you should not assume that an oncoming vehicle will give way to you. Use the Mirrors-Signal-Manoeuvre (MSM) routine and slow down to give you more time to assess the situation.

Approach at the correct speed and give yourself more time to assess and respond if you need to. Always consider what is going on behind you. It might make a difference to your actions. Meeting traffic safely depends on your use of the MSM routine.

Your instructor

Your instructor will discuss your progress and talk you through what you need to practise throughout the lesson. At first your instructor will talk you through these 'meet situations' and gradually introduce busier areas where this might occur.

■ Where a road becomes very narrow or sometimes in traffic-calming areas, priority may be designated. Circles give orders, and this sign means oncoming vehicles have priority and you must give way. Rectangles inform, so the blue sign tells you that you have priority over oncoming vehicles. However, proceed with caution and be prepared to give way if continuing might cause an accident.

At the end of each lesson your instructor will recap on what you have covered to make sure you have understood everything, and explain what the plan is for the next lesson. Your Track Record can be completed accordingly.

Accompanying driver

Explain what is to be practised and take a few moments to discuss what your learner has been taught by their instructor. Check out their Track Record which will show you how they are developing this skill.

This situation has become more common since car ownership has increased and cars are parked on the kerbside. The best place to practise this is on a quiet road primarily used for parking (as on industrial estates) or in residential areas.

Make sure you:

❑ check their knowledge and understanding of the skill

❑ personally check the mirrors before giving directions.

Make sure your learner:

❑ looks well ahead to assess the situation in good time

❑ uses the MSPSL routine

❑ slows down and is prepared to stop

❑ keeps well back from the obstruction so they can see ahead and leave room for the manoeuvre.

Advanced exercises

Practise:

a on busier roads with pedestrians and cyclists as distractions

b without prompting.

Give a recap of how they have done and praise them for their efforts, even if they have found it difficult. Discuss the session with them by asking them to assess their own performance.

Your examiner

Use the MSM routine. Care should be taken when the width of the road is restricted or when the road narrows. If there is an obstruction on your side or not enough room for two vehicles to pass safely, you should be prepared to wait and let the approaching vehicles through.

28 Crossing traffic

HIGHWAY CODE
170-178

When you turn right from a major into a minor road you usually have to cross the path of oncoming traffic. You must learn to judge how much time you need in order to make your turn safely. If you are able to anticipate a gap in the traffic, you may be able to slow down and complete your turn without ever having to stop.

If your car is still moving, you can make safe use of smaller gaps in the oncoming traffic. But once your car has stopped, you need extra time to get it moving again. Oncoming vehicles should not have to stop, slow down or swerve to allow you to complete the turn.

If the road is busy, you will often have to stop and wait for a safe gap. If this is the case, make sure you position your car correctly. This position is normally just to the left of the centre of the road. Look for gaps in the oncoming traffic.

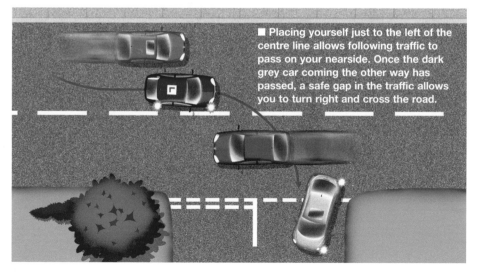

■ Placing yourself just to the left of the centre line allows following traffic to pass on your nearside. Once the dark grey car coming the other way has passed, a safe gap in the traffic allows you to turn right and cross the road.

When judging a safe gap, look at the approaching traffic and ask yourself whether you would walk across the road in front of that car. If the answer is 'yes', make your turn. If the answer is 'no' or 'I don't know', don't go.

Your instructor

Your instructor will discuss your progress and talk you through what you need to practise throughout the lesson. You will not cover this skill until your instructor is happy that you can cope with the skill and judgement it requires. You will discuss the dangers of this manoeuvre.

At the end of each lesson your instructor will recap on what you have covered to make sure you have understood everything and explain what the plan is for the next lesson. Your Track Record can be completed accordingly.

Accompanying driver

Explain what is to be practised and take a few moments to discuss what your learner has been taught by their instructor. Check out their Track Record which will show you how they are developing this skill.

Your learner needs to be able to make a right turn safely and under control, before putting them into a busy situation where they will have to cross the path of oncoming vehicles.

Make sure you:

- ❑ check their knowledge and understanding of the skill

- ❑ personally check it is safe each time before you turn right

- ❑ are especially aware that the learner may find it difficult to judge the speed of oncoming traffic and select a safe gap

- ❑ are always ready to prompt the learner to steer or, when absolutely necessary, to take control of the wheel yourself.

Make sure your learner:

- ❑ uses the mirrors effectively

- ❑ gives correct signal at an appropriate time

- ❑ takes up correct position on approach

- ❑ drives at an appropriate speed on approach

- ❑ selects the correct gear

- ❑ observes adequately on approach

- ❑ times approach to select a safe gap or give way as necessary

- ❑ takes up correct position before turning

- ❑ makes a final check of right-hand mirror

- ❑ steers sufficiently and at correct time to turn.

Advanced exercises

Practise:

a on busier roads with pedestrians and
  cyclists as distractions

b without prompting.

Give a recap of how they have done and
praise them for their efforts, even if they
have found it difficult. Discuss the session
with them by asking them to assess their
own performance.

Your examiner

When turning right, other vehicles should not
have to stop, slow down or swerve to allow
you to complete the turn. You should use the
Mirrors-Signal-Manoeuvre (MSM) routine,
position the car correctly, and complete the
turn under control.

HIGHWAY CODE
135, 160, 162-169, 230

Overtaking another moving vehicle is
potentially dangerous, particularly on single
carriageway roads where oncoming traffic will
be meeting you head on. You really need to
learn the skills of overtaking safely before
driving alone.

Do you need to overtake? Consider whether:

❏ the vehicle in front is signalling its
  intention of turning off the road

❏ you intend turning off the road shortly
  yourself

❏ there is a sign informing you that there is a
  dual carriageway in half a mile or so

❏ the driver is only travelling a couple of
  mph slower than you are – so is the risk
  worth it?

❏ you would need to exceed the speed limit
  in order to overtake.

Is it legal to overtake? Look out for road signs
and road markings. Do NOT overtake where:

❏ there is a bend in the road or on the brow
  of a hill

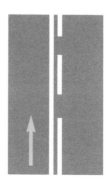

■ You may cross a double white line to
overtake where the line nearest to you is
broken, if it's safe to do so, but make sure
you can complete the manoeuvre before
reaching a solid line on your side. You may
not cross or straddle double white lines
where the one nearest to you is solid.

- you can see a junction to the left or to the right and can't be sure that someone isn't waiting to emerge

- there is oncoming traffic

- the road is not wide enough.

If you do decide to overtake, do so safely.

Position
You have decided you wish to overtake the vehicle in front because they are either slowing or you are travelling at a higher speed and reducing your separation distance. In order to make progress and overtake you should keep this distance until you are sure it is safe to overtake.

Speed
Slow down to the speed of the car and change down a gear, as you may need the power to overtake when the road is clear.

Look
Look ahead, well down the road to check that it is safe.

Mirrors
Check all around before you move out.

Signal
Your signal will show your intention to all road users, both in front and behind.

Manoeuvre
Move out smoothly and swiftly, leaving plenty of room between you and the other vehicle and making sure that you can see the vehicle in your interior mirror before you move back in to the left.

When overtaking a cyclist or motorcyclist, leave as much room as you would a car. Be aware that they can wobble or swerve around drains or potholes.

■ Check in your mirrors before moving out.

Your instructor

Your instructor will discuss your progress and talk you through what you need to practise throughout the lesson. You will not cover this skill until your instructor is happy that you can cope with the skill and judgement it requires. You will discuss the dangers of this manoeuvre.

At the end of each lesson your instructor will recap on what you have covered to make sure you have understood everything, and explain what the plan is for the next lesson. Your Track Record can be completed accordingly.

Accompanying driver

Explain what is to be practised and take a few moments to discuss what your learner has been taught by their instructor. Check out their Track Record which will show you how they are developing this skill.

Overtaking is a risky manoeuvre. Everything has to be right for it to be done safely. On single carriageways it is particularly risky and should not be practised unless the vehicle in front is holding up traffic. Make sure you:

❑ check their knowledge and understanding of the skill

❑ are personally aware of all speed limits and conditions that affect the safe overtake

❑ do not encourage your driver to make progress where it is not safe.

Make sure your learner:

❑ has the skill to cope with this manoeuvre

before practising

❑ considers whether it is necessary

❑ uses the safety routine

❑ leaves as much room as they would a car when overtaking cyclists and motorcyclists

❑ does not exceed the speed limit in order to complete the manoeuvre

❑ does not cut in on the car being overtaken.

Advanced exercises

Practise:

a on faster roads such as dual carriageways

b where your learner has to change gear in order to manoeuvre safely.

Give a recap of how they have done and praise them for their efforts, even if they have found it difficult. Discuss the session with them by asking them to assess their own performance.

Your examiner

If you overtake you need to show that you can do so safely by checking that you leave a sufficient safety margin and do not cut in too quickly after overtaking.

When overtaking cyclists and motorcyclists, you should leave them as much space as you would for other vehicles – and remember that they can wobble or swerve suddenly.

30 Awareness and planning – towns

HIGHWAY CODE
152, 153, 204-225

You need a plan of action for every possible and actual problem that arises. The earlier you can spot a possible problem, the easier you will be able to deal with it safely. You can avoid the need for a sudden action, such as harsh braking, that could endanger yourself and others.

As soon as you spot a potential problem, you must decide what action you need to take, and then respond as necessary. The faster you are travelling, the less time you have in which to do this. You will need to reduce your speed simply to give yourself more time to think.

As you drive along, you must stay alert and be looking well ahead continually and all around for any possible problems that may arise.

Every time your view is restricted or your space is reduced, slow down and give yourself more time to look and think and act.

Driving with good awareness and planning will also reduce the fuel you use by ensuring you are at the correct speed for the conditions, and therefore avoiding harsh braking and acceleration.

You should use the following Five Habits.

1. Look well ahead

Looking well ahead means looking well down the road. At the start it's very easy to forget to look well ahead and instead concentrate on the car immediately in front of you. But seeing problems further down the road will give you more time to deal with them.

Looking well ahead allows you to:

☐ see any problems early

☐ judge and adjust your speed

☐ increase your options of how to deal with a situation

☐ decide if any action is needed in good time.

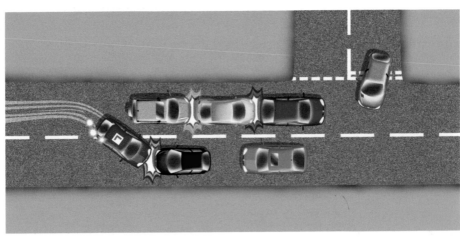

■ Looking well ahead can prevent this kind of situation from developing.

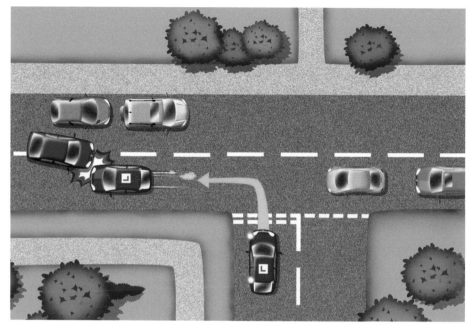

■ It's essential to keep your eyes moving at all times, otherwise you might not view the parked cars as a potential hazard. In traffic, the situation can change rapidly.

2. Move your eyes

You should keep your eyes moving all the time to the near, middle and far distance, in your mirrors and, when necessary, your blind spots. This is sometimes referred to as scanning. This should become a habit while driving. Crashes and collisions can occur due to a driver not using their eyes or moving their head to see a hazard that is not directly ahead.

3. Spot the problems

Some of the hazards you see will need a response, such as slowing down, or changing direction such as traffic lights or direction signs. Some you need to keep a mental note of – just in case the situation changes – such as children playing at the side of the road.

Are they going to run out? Will there be enough time to stop? Do you need to slow down?

4. Keep space

Space around your car can give you time to look, think, spot risks and respond. Further details of keeping space can be found in section 24.

5. Be seen

There are many ways of making yourself seen when driving – including lights, flashing lights, signals, brake lights, horn, making eye contact, keeping out of other drivers' blind spots, fog lamps and position on the road.

Being seen is your means of communication with other road users. You cannot expect others to see you, or even to make themselves adequately visible. You must make them see you, and even then you cannot entirely rely on them not to make a wrong move. Don't assume another driver or pedestrian has seen you or that your indicators give you priority.

When driving through busy town areas, there will be lots going on. Pedestrians will be wanting to cross the road, and not always concentrating on what they are doing.

Parked vehicles also provide hazards by shielding crossing pedestrians, especially children. Doors may open and the driver get out of the car into the road.

You should note the traffic and directions signs so you can deal with any changes in speed or direction in good time.

You will have to scan all around and look for the clues that tell you of a potential hazard. This will all come with experience but it is a very important part of becoming a safe driver, which is why it is also part of the Theory Test.

In towns you may have to deal with:

❑ buses/bus lanes

❑ trams

❑ pedestrians

❑ taxis

❑ unusual roundabouts

❑ cyclists

❑ over and underpasses.

Your instructor

Your instructor will discuss your progress and introduce more complex situations, such as busy shopping areas and streets with parked cars.

At the end of the lesson your instructor will recap on what you have covered to make sure you have understood everything, and explain what the plan is for the next lesson. Your Track Record can be completed accordingly.

■ Beware the hazards of parked vehicles...

Accompanying driver

Explain what is to be practised and take a few moments to discuss what your learner has been taught by their instructor. Check out their Track Record which will show you how they are developing this skill.

There is no quick way to gain experience. This is why your input is so valuable, as time on the road dealing with all different types of situation is an important part of gaining awareness and planning skills.

At first, make your visits to town areas during quieter times to give your learner the chance to deal with the situations gradually. As the traffic becomes busier, you will have to be sure that all your instructions are given in good time so that your learner is not trying to deal with hazards while also listening to your instructions. Make sure you:

❑ check their knowledge and understanding of the skill

❑ are personally aware of what is going on all around

❑ watch your learner to check for routines

❑ balance the traffic situation with the ability of your learner

❑ do not destroy their confidence by driving at a busier time than they can cope with.

Make sure your learner:

❑ is aware of what is all around

❑ uses the Mirrors-Signal-Position-Speed-Look (MSPSL) routine if they have to change speed and direction

❑ has the control and awareness skills to deal with town situations

❑ controls their speed (not too fast or too hesitant).

Advanced exercises

Practise:

a at busier times of the day

b on more complex traffic systems

c where there are other transport systems such as trams.

Give a recap of how they have done and praise them for their efforts, even if they have found it difficult. Discuss the session with them by asking them to assess their own performance.

Your examiner

You will be expected to display an awareness of and consideration for other road users at all times. You should have the ability to think and plan ahead, judging what other road users are going to do, predicting how their actions will affect the vehicle, and respond in good time.

You need to consider the actions of the more vulnerable groups of road users such as pedestrians, cyclists, motorcyclists and horse riders. Anticipate road and traffic conditions while you are driving, acting in good time, so you do not have to react to them at the last moment.

31 Awareness and planning – country roads

HIGHWAY CODE
154–156, 204-225

The principles of awareness and planning in the country are the same as in the town, but you will find different types of hazards to think about in the countryside.

Country lanes have bends and perhaps dead ground (this is the ground you cannot see when approaching a dip in the road). You need to think about what could be around the bend. There could a pedestrian, horse rider, slow-moving tractor or even a herd of sheep.

Other hazards you need to think about are:

❏ roads without pavements

❏ farm entrances

❏ mud or wet leaves on the road

❏ uneven roads.

Your instructor

Your instructor will discuss your progress and explain to you the potential hazards of the countryside – such as separation distances, the dangers of overtaking on roads with bends, and how to use passing places.

At the end of the lesson your instructor will recap on what you have covered to make sure you have understood everything and explain what the plan is for the next lesson. Your Track Record can be completed accordingly.

Accompanying driver

Explain what is to be practised and take a few moments to discuss what your learner has been taught by their instructor. Check out their Track Record which will show you how they are developing this skill.

You might think that, when choosing a place to start to learn to drive, a country road is ideal. That is not necessarily the case. There are many hidden dangers and you must both be aware of them and plan accordingly.

Make sure you:

❏ check their knowledge and understanding of the skill

❏ think about the potential hazards of country driving

❏ personally be aware of what is going on all around you

❏ prompt your learner if you feel they are going too fast for the conditions.

Make sure your learner:

❏ is aware of what is all around

❏ uses the Mirrors-Signal-Position-Speed-Look (MSPSL) routine if they have to change speed and direction

❏ is aware of the potential hazards which country driving brings

❏ makes progress but adjusts their speed according to the conditions or potential hazards.

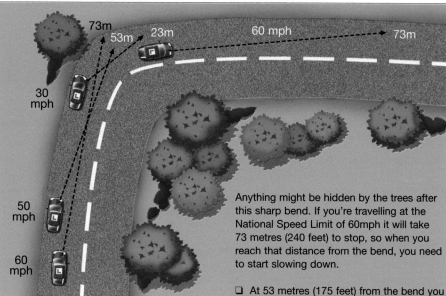

73m
53m 23m
60 mph
73m

30
mph

50
mph

60
mph

Anything might be hidden by the trees after this sharp bend. If you're travelling at the National Speed Limit of 60mph it will take 73 metres (240 feet) to stop, so when you reach that distance from the bend, you need to start slowing down.

❏ At 53 metres (175 feet) from the bend you need to be doing no more that 50mph or risk hitting a concealed hazard.

❏ At 23 metres (75 feet) your maximum speed will need to be 30mph, or you are in trouble.

❏ On reaching the bend, you can see that the road is clear. You can now pick up your speed back to 60mph because the distance you can see to be clear ahead exceeds 73 metres.

Advanced exercises

Practise:

a on roads with sharp bends

b at busier times of the day.

Discuss the session with them by asking them to assess their own performance.

Your examiner

You will be expected to display an awareness of and consideration for other road users at all times. You should have the ability to think and plan ahead, judging what other road users are going to do, predicting how their actions will affect the vehicle, and respond in good time.

You need to consider the dangers that country driving brings, such as horse riders. Anticipate road and traffic conditions while you are driving, acting in good time, so you do not have to react to them at the last moment.

32 Lane discipline and positioning

HIGHWAY CODE
131, 133-143, 151, 184-187, 228

The basic rule is to keep to the left unless you are overtaking or turning right.

You should position your car so that you don't interfere with oncoming traffic, but not too close to the left-hand kerb. The bumps and drains in the gutter make steering control difficult but, more importantly, you will be too close to pedestrians and have less time to react if they step into the road.

You should be about a metre from the kerb. This is very flexible because on some narrow roads, a metre could mean you were crossing the centre line. Traffic ahead may turn right. Be ready to go through on the left if there is room. After passing obstructions in the road, return to the left. Do not weave in and out of frequent obstructions. Maintain a steady course.

Where there are lanes:

❏ drive in the middle of your lane

❏ select the lane for the direction you intend to take

❏ watch out for filter lanes at traffic lights.

You should aim to take the lane closest to the left for the direction in which you want to go.

For example, imagine you are approaching a major set of lights and wish to turn right. There are five lanes on the approach. One has a left-turn arrow, the next two have straight-ahead arrows and the next two have right-turn arrows. You should select the left-hand lane of the two right-hand lanes. In this way, once you have turned right you will finish up in the left-hand lane of the new road.

When driving you should:

❏ normally keep to the left

■ Driving too close to the kerb can be dangerous to pedestrians, and the drains can make steering control difficult.

■ Use your judgement on narrow roads – being the proper metre from the kerb or edge may put you over the centre line.

- avoid weaving in and out between parked cars

- obey lane markings

- select the appropriate lane in good time using the Mirrors-Signal-Position-Speed-Look (MSPSL) routine.

Passing stationary vehicles

Cars might be parked in most side roads; even on main roads, delivery vehicles and buses will be stopped at the side of the road. You must allow plenty of room when passing stationary vehicles. Look well ahead to spot any vehicles parked that might force you to change direction. Allow, if possible, the width of a car door.

Where there is less space, you need less speed to allow you more time to react should someone open a car door. Look for people sitting in the driver's seat, but remember that you cannot look into every parked car, so leave enough room anyway.

Another reason for leaving a car door's width between you and parked cars is that a child could run out into the road. Look for feet under the cars and, again, be ready to stop. Watch out for a cyclist who may pull out around a parked car without looking or stopping. And watch out for people coming out in front of a bus at a bus stop.

Your instructor

Your instructor will discuss your progress and talk you through what you need to practise throughout the lesson. You will learn the importance of positioning your car correctly and selecting and maintaining your position within lanes. At the end of each lesson your instructor will recap on what you have covered to make sure you have understood everything and explain what the plan is for the next lesson. Your Track Record can be completed accordingly.

■ At road junctions with several lanes, select the left-hand lane of the two right-hand lanes in order to end up on the left-hand lane of the new road.

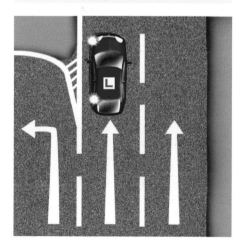

■ Watch out for filter lanes, because they may be the only possibility to make a turn. If you're stuck, carry on and find another way to continue your journey.

101

Accompanying driver

Explain what is to be practised and take a few moments to discuss what your learner has been taught by their instructor. Check out their Track Record which will show you how they are developing this skill.

Some learners find positioning their vehicle on the road easier than others. If they have been a cyclist or moped rider, they can take time to get used to the different view of the road.

In the beginning, find a quiet road where they can get used to this and gradually introduce busier roads as their control and awareness skills improve.

Make sure you:

- [ ] check their knowledge and understanding of the skill

- [ ] personally check it is safe each time before making any change of direction such as a lane change

- [ ] prompt if necessary.

Make sure your learner:

- [ ] allows a width of a car door when passing stationary vehicles

- [ ] keeps to the left normally

- [ ] obeys any road markings

- [ ] changes direction safely using MSPSL routine

- [ ] maintains their position in the correct lane.

Advanced exercises

Practise:

a on busier roads and junctions

b unprompted.

Give a recap of how they have done and praise them for their efforts, even if they have found it difficult. Discuss the session with them by asking them to assess their own performance.

Your examiner

Drive with an understanding of the room needed when passing stationary vehicles and obstructions. Show awareness and readiness to be prepared to slow down or stop, if a door opens or a child runs out without warning.

You should be positioned correctly for your intended route. Where lanes are marked, you should be positioned to the middle of the lane. Straddling lane markings should be avoided and you should not change lanes unnecessarily.

33 One-way systems

HIGHWAY CODE
143

With the increasing traffic on the roads, towns and cities are constantly trying to update their road systems. One-way systems are becoming more common as the attempt to keep traffic moving is addressed.

You should be able to recognise the signs that indicate a one-way street such as:

No Entry (one-way in the opposite direction)

One-way street

Turn left only

Vehicles may pass either side (of a traffic island) to reach the same destination

Two-way traffic straight ahead

Two-way traffic crosses one-way road

On a one-way system you are permitted to use either lane; however, you need to plan well ahead and choose the most appropriate lane for the route you are going to take. You need to keep a lookout for all the direction signs and make sure you leave plenty of time to make your exit or turn at a junction without changing lanes at the last moment.

Your instructor

Your instructor will discuss your progress and talk you through what you need to practise throughout the lesson. You will be given the opportunity to learn about one-way streets and taken to any local areas that will allow you to practise.

Remember, once you have passed your test, you will be able to drive in any big city, so it is important that you understand all the signs and procedures you need to take.

At the end of the lesson your instructor will recap on what you have covered to make sure you have understood everything and explain what the plan is for the next lesson. Your Track Record can be completed accordingly.

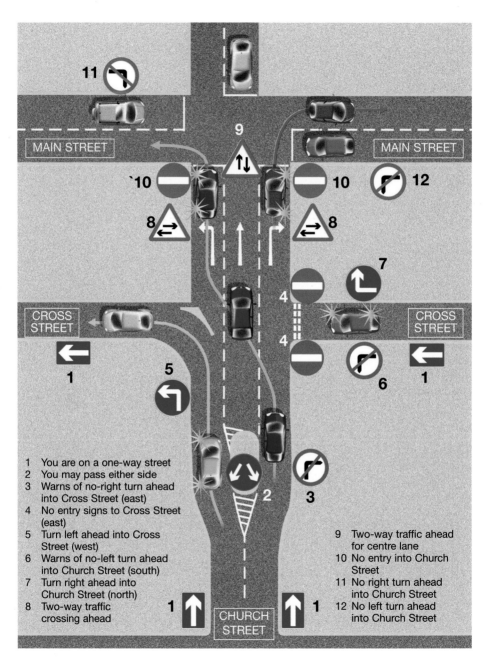

1 You are on a one-way street
2 You may pass either side
3 Warns of no-right turn ahead into Cross Street (east)
4 No entry signs to Cross Street (east)
5 Turn left ahead into Cross Street (west)
6 Warns of no-left turn ahead into Church Street (south)
7 Turn right ahead into Church Street (north)
8 Two-way traffic crossing ahead

9 Two-way traffic ahead for centre lane
10 No entry into Church Street
11 No right turn ahead into Church Street
12 No left turn ahead into Church Street

Accompanying driver

Explain what is to be practised and take a few moments to discuss what your learner has been taught by their instructor. Check out their Track Record which will show you how they are developing this skill.

You will need to judge, after discussion with the instructor, whether your learner is ready for busy urban areas. One-way streets tend to be rat-runs and therefore quite busy.

Make sure you:

❏ check their knowledge and understanding of the skill

❏ are aware of all the relevant road signs

❏ give your instruction in good time and prompt your learner to get into the correct lane if necessary

❏ personally check it is safe when emerging or changing lanes.

Make sure your learner:

❏ understands all the relevant road signs

❏ uses the mirrors effectively

❏ gives correct signals at an appropriate time

❏ takes up correct position on the road and at approach to a junction

❏ adjusts speed appropriately on approach

❏ observes before/during emerging positions correctly for the turn or exit being taken.

Advanced exercises

Practise:

a on busier roads and gyratory systems

b allow your learner to forward plan their own route and position through the one-way system.

Give a recap of how they have done and praise them for their efforts, even if they have found it difficult. Discuss the session with them by asking them to assess their own performance.

Your examiner

If you are taken on a one-way road during your test your examiner will expect you to use either lane, or the appropriate lane for the route you are going to take. You will be given instruction in good time for you to change lanes safety if necessary.

34 Dual carriageways

HIGHWAY CODE
124, 137–138

As more towns are by-passed, the more you will find yourself on dual carriageways. Some carry a large amount of slow traffic and some are similar to motorways.

If there is a slip road you should adjust your speed to that of the main carriageway and look for a gap in the traffic. A quick glance to the right might be required as well as a mirror check. Only emerge if it is clear; don't force any other driver to slow down or change course.

As you are travelling at a faster speed you must use your planning and awareness skills to ensure you:

❑ keep a safe separation distance; remember the two-second rule

❑ act on all signs, signals and road markings.

You need to be looking in the near, middle and far distance.

When taking an exit you should get into the left-hand lane in good time. Looking out for signs as you drive should allow you to do this. Use the Mirrors-Signal-Manoeuvre (MSM) routine in good time, because of the higher speed.

If you have cruise control, consider using it on higher-speed roads as this can significantly reduce fuel consumption.

■ Be in the left-hand lane to take an exit in plenty of time.

Your instructor

Your instructor will discuss your progress and introduce more complex situations and higher-speed roads as you develop. You will cover joining the dual carriageway and develop your observation skills, decision making and the correct action to take.

At the end of the lesson your instructor will recap on what you have covered to make sure you have understood everything, and explain what the plan is for the next lesson. Your Track Record can be completed accordingly.

Accompanying driver

Explain what is to be practised and take a few moments to discuss what your learner has been taught by their instructor. Check out their Track Record which will show you how they are developing this skill.

It is safest to start by finding a dual carriageway that is not too busy and with two lanes in each direction. Initially, choose a place to join where there is an acceleration lane and a place to leave where there is a deceleration lane. This makes it much easier for the learner to practise joining and leaving.

Your learner may have had very limited practise to date of travelling at speeds of up to 70mph; you need to be even more vigilant than usual.

If your learner has difficulty staying in lane, end the practice as soon as it is safe; this may be due to the change from the instructor's car to yours. Make sure you:

❏ check their knowledge and understanding of the skill

- ❏ make frequent checks in your extra mirror, especially before asking the learner to change lanes, turn left or right, or overtake

- ❏ personally check the blind spot before changing lanes

- ❏ start by finding a dual carriageway, that is not too busy and with two lanes in either direction

- ❏ do not allow the learner to drive too close to the vehicle in front.

Make sure your learner:

- ❏ uses any slip roads appropriately to join or leave

- ❏ joins and leaves safely where there is no slip road

- ❏ drives in the centre of the lane

- ❏ complies with lane discipline

- ❏ keeps adequate space all around and especially in front

- ❏ uses MSM to change lanes

- ❏ changes lanes smoothly

- ❏ overtakes safely if required

- ❏ does not drive too slowly and hold up the traffic, nor break the speed limit

- ❏ uses cruise control if available and appropriate.

Advanced exercises

Practise:

a joining and leaving where there are no acceleration or deceleration lanes

b turning right onto a dual carriageway where there is a wide central reservation

c turning right onto a dual carriageway where there is a narrow central reservation

d in the dark and in bad weather.

Give a recap of how they have done and praise them for their efforts, even if they have found it difficult. Discuss the session with them by asking them to assess their own performance.

Your examiner

Your examiner will want to see you keeping up with the other traffic and making progress. You should show that you understand the signs, signals and procedures by driving safely and confidently. You should keep a safe separation distance from the vehicle in front.

■ Dual carriageway ends sign.

35 Eco-friendly driving

HIGHWAY CODE
123

The evidence of climate change and the dangers of pollution make it very important for all of us to become aware of our personal contributions. As a driver you will be contributing to this pollution – however, there are some actions and methods you can use to reduce your impact.

- If you are using your car for short journeys, consider whether you could walk or cycle instead.

- A cold engine uses more fuel.

- Early recognition of potential hazards will mean that you are travelling at the correct speed. This will help avoid harsh braking or acceleration and avoid unnecessary stopping.

- The accelerator needs to be used smoothly and progressively; when appropriate, take your foot off the accelerator and allow the momentum of the car to take you forward.

- Exceeding a speed limit by only a few mph will mean that you will use much more fuel. On fast roads, consider the appropriateness of the optimum travelling speed – 56mph in top gear. This uses 25 percent less fuel than at 70mph.

- It's not always necessary to change up or down through each gear, so you can skip gears. As soon as conditions allow, you need to use the highest possible gear, without making the engine struggle.

- With your foot fully off the accelerator, the engine needs very little fuel – so you can take advantage of engine braking when possible.

- Modern engines are very sophisticated and deliver power even when the revs are low. Make use of higher gears at lower speeds.

- Use cruise control, if available. Keeping a sustained even speed reduces fuel consumption.

- Remove unnecessary luggage from your car and remove a roof rack if not in use.

- If you don't really need to, do not drive at busy times of the day. Make appointments so that you are not stuck in traffic and therefore expensively running the engine when stationary.

- Plan your journey before you leave home so that you do not waste fuel getting lost or taking a longer route.

- When parking, reverse in – manoeuvring when the engine is cold uses a lot of fuel, so this way you can drive out easily.

- If you're lucky enough to have your own car, you should keep it in a well-maintained condition. This will reduce its emissions and fuel consumption.

Your instructor

Your instructor is aware of their role in ensuring that you learn to drive with an eco-safe attitude. You will be shown how to apply the good habits to every part of your driving, especially planning and awareness.

At the end of the lesson your instructor will recap on what you have covered to make sure you have understood everything and explain what the plan is for the next lesson. Your Track Record can be completed accordingly.

Accompanying driver

Explain what is to be practised and take a few moments to discuss what your learner has been taught by their instructor. Check out their Track Record which will show you how they are developing this skill.

Before you begin to accompany your learner you need to assess your own driving to ensure you are doing so in an eco-friendly way. It might be an idea to talk to the instructor and maybe book an hour of tuition. It might mean a whole driving style change for you.

This eco-awareness should be applied throughout the learning process, but particularly in the use of the controls and planning and awareness.

Make sure you:

❏ have knowledge and understanding of the skill

❏ check the learner's knowledge and understanding of the skill

❏ demonstrate this in your own driving.

Make sure your learner:

❏ avoids revving the engine excessively

❏ selects the correct speed for the road conditions to avoid harsh braking

❏ takes their foot from the accelerator to slow down rather than habitually using the foot brake

❏ is aware of the impact that drivers can have on the environment.

Advanced exercises

Practise:

a planning routes

b repeating routes and setting targets or fuel consumption.

Give a recap of how they have done and praise them for their efforts, even if they have found it difficult. Discuss the session with them by asking them to assess their own performance.

Your examiner

You should drive efficiently, showing an understanding of planning and awareness that will allow you to deal with situations in good time. This will result in a smooth, safe and economical drive.

36 Night driving

HIGHWAY CODE
125, 163, 248-250

The chances of being involved in an accident are greater in the dark than in daylight. You cannot see as far or as much at night, and you receive far less information about your surroundings. It's harder to judge both speed and distance, and driving at night is more of a strain. From dusk to dawn you must rely on lights to see and to be seen.

Driving at night can be a great strain on your eyes. As you get older, your eyesight is likely to alter. Such changes tend to take place so gradually that you are unlikely to notice them. The only way you can be sure your vision is adequate is to have your eyesight checked regularly, preferably by visiting a qualified optician.

■ Having a clean windscreen might seem an obvious advantage, but don't forget that dirty lights – front and rear – are not very effective when driving at night.

When you drive in the dark:

❑ don't use sunglasses or tinted glasses – they reduce your vision

❑ keep your windscreen clean – you will see better and be less dazzled by other vehicles' lights

❑ check that all your lights are working and that they are clean and properly adjusted – the effectiveness of your lights is greatly reduced if they are dirty

❑ if you are tired – don't drive.

111

You should make sure that you can see and be seen by other road users. So it is best to use headlights on all roads. In towns where there is street lighting, use dipped headlights. Sidelights are not enough and make it difficult for other drivers and pedestrians to see that you are there.

Night stopping distances

You must be able to stop within the distance you can see to be clear. Remember that, at night, this means being able to stop well within the limits of your lighting.

On an unlit road, headlights on full beam allow you to see approximately 100 metres (328 feet) ahead and dipped headlights allow you to see about 40 metres (130 feet) ahead.

Reflective road studs, however, make driving on roads equipped with them much easier. They help you to follow the course of the road ahead as your headlights pick them out.

Dealing with other traffic

The lights of another vehicle usually tell you its direction of travel but little about its speed. Decide if you need to slow down and look for any obstructions in the road ahead.

Dip your headlights to avoid dazzling oncoming drivers. Do not dip so soon that you cannot see the road ahead. Do not stare at the oncoming headlights, but look slightly towards the left-hand edge of your dipped beams. Be ready to stop if necessary.

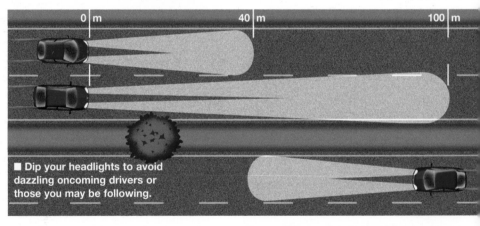

■ Dip your headlights to avoid dazzling oncoming drivers or those you may be following.

These figures are only approximations because the type of car you are driving, and the angle of the beam of light, alters the distance you can see with the headlights. But these figures should help you appreciate just how much less you can see in the dark than in the daylight.

Pedestrians and cyclists are difficult to see in the dark. They don't always wear reflective clothing, and cyclists do not always have good working lights.

Dip your lights earlier when going around a left-hand bend. Your headlight beams will sweep across eyes of anyone coming towards you. If the oncoming driver fails to dip theie lights and dazzles you, slow down and stop if necessary.

When you are following other vehicles at night, remember that your headlights on full beam can dazzle the driver in front as much as they can an oncoming vehicle. It is really disorientating to be dazzled by the vehicle

behind you, and it becomes quite impossible to focus properly on the road ahead when there is a bright light in your interior mirror filling your eyes.

So dip your lights if you are following another vehicle and keep far enough back that your dipped beams fall clear of the rear window.

Extra care is needed if you overtake at night. It is much harder to judge space and distance and the speed of other vehicles in the dark. Dangers are far more likely to be hidden from view. You cannot see properly beyond the range of your headlights.

Bends or dips in the road may conceal parked or approaching vehicles. Cyclists and pedestrians may be hidden in the gloom.

If you need to warn of your presence at night, flash your headlights. It is illegal to use your horn when driving in a built-up area between the hours of 11.30pm and 07.00am.

Your instructor

It is advisable to have at least one lesson in the dark if possible, even before your driving test. Your instructor will discuss your progress and talk you through what you need to practise throughout the lesson.

You will discuss and cover several points about the extra dangers of dealing with hazards in the dark, as well as the use of lights when driving at dusk, at night and at dawn. Speed and stopping distances will be covered as your judgement can be affected in darkness. What to do if others dazzle you will also be discussed.

At the end of the lesson your instructor will recap on what you have covered to make sure you have understood everything, and explain what the plan is for the next lesson. Your Track Record can be completed accordingly.

Accompanying driver

Explain what is to be practised and take a few moments to discuss what your learner has been taught by their instructor. Check out their Track Record which will show you how they are developing this skill.

This practice session is divided into two tasks. The first involves practising driving at dusk and at night, in built-up areas and on other roads where there is street lighting. Try to plan a route that involves a variety of well-lit main roads and more poorly-lit back streets.

The second task requires the learner to practise driving on unlit roads. Plan a suitable route to include major two-way roads, dual carriageways and narrower country lanes. At least one session for each element should start just before dusk, so that the learner can decide when to turn on the headlights and become familiar with the

difficulty of seeing other vehicles that have no lights switched on.

Make sure you:

❏ check their knowledge and understanding of the skill

❏ remind the learner to turn on the headlights if they fail to do so when necessary

❏ do not allow the learner to dazzle other drivers

❏ be ready to steady the wheel if the learner is dazzled by oncoming traffic

❏ pay particular attention to speed, especially when passing oncoming traffic and approaching bends

❏ watch out for cyclists and pedestrians

who may be hidden in the gloom

☐ take care at junctions where the speed of other traffic may be hard to judge.

Make sure your learner:

☐ switches on dipped headlights when required

☐ uses full-beam headlights on unlit roads when safe to do so

☐ avoids dazzling other road users and dips the lights when necessary and at the right moment

☐ adjusts speed to match conditions and visibility

☐ judges the speed of other traffic accurately

☐ judges space and distance accurately

☐ takes appropriate action when dazzled by another vehicle.

Advanced exercises

Practise:

a on roads with faster-moving traffic

b on country roads with bends

c in heavy traffic.

Give a recap of how they have done and praise them for their efforts, even if they have found it difficult. Discuss the session with them by asking them to assess their own performance.

Your examiner

It is unlikely that you will take your driving test in the dark, but adverse weather conditions could cause gloom. It is important you know about night driving, as your licence, when you receive it, will allow you to drive in the dark unaccompanied.

■ Headlight dazzle can be a problem.

37 Bad weather

HIGHWAY CODE
93–94, 213, 226–237, 251, Annex 6

Driving in the United Kingdom can mean that you need to get used to driving in all sorts of weather conditions, each bringing with it its own dangers.

Wet weather

❏ Increase your separation distance; it can take twice the distance to stop

❏ Know how and when to use the de-mister

❏ Top up the washer bottle

❏ Use dipped headlights if there is poor visibility

❏ Reduce your speed accordingly.

You need to be aware of the dangers of aquaplaning. This occurs when a film of water builds up between the road surface and your tyres, which then lose all contact with the road. This can cause the steering to become very light. If this happens you need to ease off the accelerator – don't try to brake or steer harshly.

Spray from other vehicles can also be a problem, so reduce your speed to suit the conditions.

■ **Two signs to watch out for in bad weather: risk of ice (left) and potential for skidding in wet, snowy or icy conditions.**

Ice and snow

Increase your separation distance – it can take ten times the distance to stop.

❏ Clear the windscreen and windows of frost or snow

❏ Use the de-mister and heater, but do not drive off until the screen is clear

❏ Avoid harsh braking

❏ If the roads are very icy, consider whether you need to travel at all.

Fog

Fog is dangerous because it is unpredictable. It sometimes appears in patches and the density can vary.

❏ Use your dipped headlights and/or fog lights.

❏ Use high-intensity rear lights if visibility is reduced to less than 100 metres (328 feet). (Don't forget to switch them off when it is clear.)

Remember, you must be able to stop well within the distance you can see to be clear, so don't 'hang on' to the lights of the vehicle in front too closely.

Sunshine

This can be problem, especially in the winter when the sun is low. Use the sun visor and use quality sunglasses to reduce the glare. You should also be prepared for the heat, so make sure you:

❑ ventilate the car

❑ drink plenty of liquid

❑ stop if you are feeling tired

❑ top up your car radiator.

Your instructor

It may not be possible to experience all possible adverse weather conditions on your lessons. However, your instructor will talk you through the dangers, causes and prevention of skidding.

At the end of the lesson your instructor will recap on what you have covered to make sure you have understood everything, and explain what the plan is for the next lesson. Your Track Record can be completed accordingly.

Accompanying driver

Practising with learners in bad weather can be highly dangerous. Learners should only be accompanied by an approved driving instructor in a dual-controlled car in poor weather conditions. Even then, the conditions may be too dangerous to allow tuition to continue.

In consequence it is **strongly recommended** that you do not accompany a learner to practise in adverse weather conditions, other than rain.

In the case of rainy weather, explain what is to be practised and take a few moments to discuss what your learner has been taught by their instructor. Check out their Track Record which will show you how they are developing this skill.

Practising in any other type of bad weather should not be conducted until the learner has passed the Practical Driving Test and has gained some experience as a newly qualified driver in good weather conditions.

Whenever possible, the newly qualified driver should undertake a practical lesson with an approved driving instructor in each bad-weather scenario, before undertaking practice with an accompanying driver.

The weather forecast may allow you to plan a bad-weather practice session. You may equally need to seize the opportunity when it arises. In the case of rain and fog, you should plan a route that includes a variety of different types of road, both in and out of town. In snow and ice, it is safest to practise car control skills in a large car park or very quiet side roads before driving in traffic.

Practise:

❑ on unlit roads where there are a series of hills and bends

❑ on country roads where there are no reflective road studs

❑ reversing in the dark on both lit and unlit roads

❑ on a narrow country lane with passing places

❑ overtaking on unlit roads.

Make sure you:

❏ consider whether the conditions are too extreme

❏ ensure your car is adequately prepared for the journey

❏ carry appropriate safety equipment.

Make sure your learner:

❏ checks and prepares the car for the journey

❏ uses lights correctly and turns them off when no longer needed

❏ uses windscreen wipers, washer and de-mister as needed

❏ drives at an appropriate speed and keeps a safe distance from the vehicle in front

❏ makes gentle use of the controls and uses appropriate gears for the conditions.

Advanced exercises

Advanced exercises, except in the rain, are too dangerous to practise on a public road.

Practise in the rain:

a on dual carriageways where spray from large vehicles causes problems.

b at night.

Give a recap of how they have done and praise them for their efforts, even if they have found it difficult. Discuss the session with them by asking them to assess their own performance.

Your examiner

If the weather is very bad, then your test will not take place. However, you may have to deal with heavy rain or low sun. You will be expected to drive at the appropriate speed for the conditions and be able to locate any ancillary controls required such as wipers and de-misters.

38 Commentary driving

Driving while giving a commentary is a great way to assess your own planning and awareness skills. It can take practice and it does not suit everyone. If you feel it is distracting you from concentrating perhaps it is not for you.

Talking yourself through your driving can improve your perception of what is happening on the road.

Better perception should increase awareness and improve our judgement of speeds, distances and timings. Improved judgements reduce the accident risk and therefore improve road safety.

At first, appearing to talk to yourself could make you feel self conscious and can lower your travelling speed, but practice will help you overcome this. Take a deep breath and start your commentary by concentrating on what you consider the major hazard(s) ahead.

Prioritise 'fixed features' such as junctions and pedestrian crossings, 'moving features' such as traffic and pedestrians, and the 'weather' and its effect on the road surface.

Aim your vision as high and as forward as you can to prevent your commentary becoming retrospective.

Use short positive statements such as:

- ❏ Roundabout – I intend to turn right

- ❏ Mirrors – clear / one following / one closing

- ❏ Signal – checking any traffic reaction

- ❏ Position – left of centre / hazard line

- ❏ Speed – gentle braking / appropriate gear selected to...

- ❏ Look – Proceed into safe break in traffic on roundabout.

With perseverance your commentary will flow naturally.

Your instructor

Your instructor will discuss your progress and decide when it is time to introduce this skill. Every learner is different, but generally your instructor will demonstrate the skill. Listen, and you will come to understand the thought processes behind each manoeuvre. With your instructor still driving, you can give the commentary, so you get used to the process. If you are happy, you can then drive and your instructor can commentate.

In the last stage you drive and commentate. This will only be for short periods of time so you get used to the method.

Commentary driving is not for everyone – some learners feel self-conscious when talking out loud. However, it is a really good way of assessing your own driving and improving your planning and awareness skills.

Accompanying driver

It is advisable that you practise this yourself, before taking this session. You may find it useful to ask the instructor for some practical advice.

It is a very good way of establishing what your learner is looking at and how they prioritise what they see. At the start, plan a short route and commentate for about five minutes. Repeat the same route several times. Make sure you:

- check their knowledge and understanding of the skill

- don't become distracted by your learner's commentary

- are aware that when the learner is driving and giving a commentary, their driving may suffer initially from the extra mental effort needed

- start by simply asking the learner to point out risks they can see, then gradually build on this so that they also predict potential problems, and finally include what action they are taking

- keep the exercise short and simple at the start.

Make sure your learner:

- looks well ahead for possible problems

- selects appropriate problems on which to comment

- proposes actions which are safe, well-timed and appropriate

- maintains a high level of concentration

- demonstrates all-round awareness throughout their commentary

- maintains control of the car to a reasonably high standard.

Advanced exercises

Practise:

a for longer periods of time as concentration improves

b by increasing the amount of detail in the commentary

c on country roads

d in the dark.

Give a recap of how they have done and praise them for their efforts, even if they have found it difficult. Discuss the session with them by asking them to assess their own performance.

Your examiner

You will not be asked to give a commentary drive on your test. However, the improvement it can make to your planning and awareness skills will help raise the standard of your overall driving skills.

39 Reversing in a straight line

HIGHWAY CODE
200, 202, 203, 206, 263

It's a good idea to practise reversing in a straight line before you attempt to reverse around a corner. You will find that only tiny movements of the steering wheel are necessary in order to keep the car straight.

Looking backwards can seem strange and may cause you to turn the steering wheel in the opposite direction. Try to focus on an object a long way down the road behind the car. This will help you to judge whether you are travelling in a straight line. Your view to the rear is more restricted than when looking forwards, so it's important that you do not just rely on the view of your mirrors to tell you what is happening behind. Ensure that you look over your shoulder through the rear window and that you are prepared to give way to anything that might be in your path.

It might feel uncomfortable and awkward to look over your left shoulder for any length of time, so alter your position in the seat. Turn in the seat so that your body and not just your head is to the left. In this position you need to check that you can still reach the pedals easily.

You may now find it easier to hold the wheel with your right hand at the top and your left hand at the bottom. If you find this awkward, you may also rest your left hand on the back of the passenger seat or on the edge of your seat and reverse with just one hand on the wheel.

The most important things are that you can

■ Turn in your seat so that your body as well as your head is to the left. If necessary, you may support the position by placing the left arm over the passenger seat back.

see well through the rear windscreen and that you can maintain this view throughout the manoeuvre, while maintaining full control of the car.

Your instructor

Your instructor will discuss your progress and talk you through what you need to practise throughout the lesson.

You will practise reversing in a straight line before moving on to the other reverse manoeuvres; this will be done in a quiet place so you are not distracted by other road users, or cause an obstruction. You will learn about co-ordination of the controls and steering, observation, speed and the potential risks.

At the end of the lesson your instructor will recap on what you have covered to make sure you have understood everything, and explain what the plan is for the next lesson. Your Track Record can be completed accordingly.

Accompanying driver

Explain what is to be practised and take a few moments to discuss what your learner has been taught by their instructor. Check out their Track Record which will show you how they are developing this skill.

Before you start this session, find a quiet, level road that's reasonably wide to allow the learner to deviate from their course safely.

Make sure you:

❑ check their knowledge and understanding of the skill

❑ avoid any road where children are playing

❑ personally check that it is safe before moving off

❑ keep looking all around as the car starts to move

❑ look for traffic both front and rear

❑ are aware that the learner may get confused with the steering as they turn to face the rear.

Make sure your learner:

❑ looks all around before the car moves

❑ waits for any traffic to pass

❑ makes appropriate observation to check it is safe throughout the manoeuvre

❑ controls the speed

❑ steers gently without harsh movements

❑ maintains a straight course

❑ maintains control

❑ avoids touching the kerb

❑ parks safely at the end of the manoeuvre.

Advanced exercises

Straight-line reversing exercises are intended to prepare your learner for reversing around a corner, so the next stage is to move onto that next key skill covered in the following sessions.

Give a recap of how they have done and praise them for their efforts, even if they have found it difficult. Discuss the session with them by asking them to assess their own performance.

Your examiner

Although this will not be a specific exercise, you never know what situation might occur on your test. If this occasion occurs you should show you can control the vehicle accurately whilst reversing and use effective all-round observation throughout, showing consideration to other road users.

40 Sharp left reverse

HIGHWAY CODE
200–203, 206, 263

Reversing is part of everyday driving, but it does carry a high risk. This is because your view from the driver's seat is restricted and your position in the seat is not as comfortable as when facing forward. Check out the advice given in the previous session.

Before you reverse, first consider the following points:

- ❏ Do you need to reverse around the corner? It might be safer to drive on and find a roundabout or to drive around the block, especially if you are in a busy road.

- ❏ Are there pedestrians about? Take a good look to the rear and wait – there could be a child behind you in the blind spot.

- ❏ The front of your car will sweep out into the road as you reverse around the corner – will this hold up traffic?

When reversing:

- ❏ look into the turning to check it's suitable

- ❏ stop about 40 centimetres (16 inches) away from the kerb and at least two-plus car lengths beyond the corner; make sure you are parallel to the kerb and that you stop with the wheels straight

- ❏ take a look all around before reversing

- ❏ keep the car under full control (at about walking pace)

- ❏ keep reasonably close to the kerb while looking out for other traffic and pedestrians, particularly children, who may be hidden behind the car (if necessary, get out and look).

123

❏ look in the direction of travel but also make frequent checks forward to see what the situation is and whether there is any need to give way to other road users, including pedestrians.

You may find it easier if you think about this in three parts:

Reverse to the point of turn
At the start, look well down the road and note where the kerb cuts into the rear windscreen. If you keep the kerb in relation to the rear windscreen in the same place, then the car will remain on a straight course.

Point of turn
The point of turn is where the rear wheel nearest the kerb lines up with the start of the corner – the first curved kerbstone. However,

you will not be able to see this, so you need to identify something that indicates you're at this point. There are several methods and you need to discuss with your instructor which one suits you best.

Make good all-round observation and apply the full left-hand lock to the steering while keeping the car moving at a walking pace. You need to keep looking as you turn and respond safely to what you see. You might have to stop and let another vehicle pass. Remember, the front of your car will sweep out.

Looking through the rear windscreen, note when the kerb lines cut into the screen again, just as they did at the start. This should indicate when you are almost parallel with the kerb and you need to straighten the wheels.

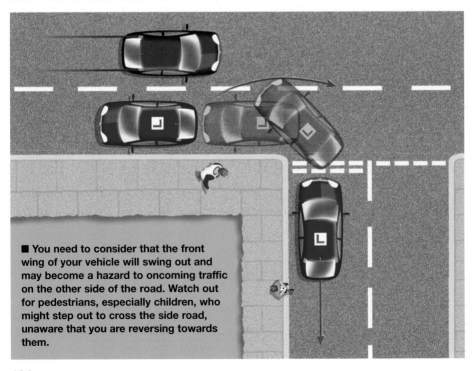

■ **You need to consider that the front wing of your vehicle will swing out and may become a hazard to oncoming traffic on the other side of the road. Watch out for pedestrians, especially children, who might step out to cross the side road, unaware that you are reversing towards them.**

Reverse into the new road

Keep reversing at walking pace, looking through the rear windscreen to check the position of the kerb. Keep checking all around and stop and give way to any other cars you might be obstructing. You need to stop about three car lengths into the road and reasonably close to the kerb.

Your instructor

Your instructor will discuss your progress and talk you through what you need to practise throughout the lesson. You will learn about co-ordination of the controls and steering, observation, speed and the potential risks.

At the end of the lesson your instructor will recap on what you have covered to make sure you have understood everything, and explain what the plan is for the next lesson. Your Track Record can be completed accordingly.

Accompanying driver

Explain what is to be practised and take a few moments to discuss what your learner has been taught by their instructor – particularly that the learner can reverse slowly in a straight line, for a reasonable distance – before you attempt this exercise. Check out their Track Record which will show you how they are developing this skill.

Find a quiet junction where the roads are level, with no parked cars in the vicinity of the corner around which the learner will practise reversing. The corner should be reasonably sharp (nearly a right angle).

Stop in the major road before the corner around which the learner is going to reverse.

This allows them to assess the corner and then to drive past it and stop in a suitable position to start the practice. Make sure you:

- ❏ check their knowledge and understanding of the skill

- ❏ avoid corners where a tree or post-box is near the kerb or obstructs their view

- ❏ avoid any road junctions where children are playing

- ❏ personally check that it is safe just before the car starts to reverse

- ❏ keep checking all around as the car starts to move

- ❏ check particularly for oncoming traffic as the learner begins to steer because the front of the car will swing out.

Make sure your learner:

- ❏ positions safely and suitably in order to commence the reverse

- ❏ looks into the turning for any problems

- ❏ prepares to reverse correctly, including their seating position and grip on the steering wheel

- ❏ looks all around before the car moves

- ❏ looks back over left shoulder while reversing in a straight line towards the corner with frequent glances to the front

- ❏ checks all round before steering and especially over right shoulder before the front of the car

- ❏ gives way to other traffic or pedestrians.

Advanced exercises

Practise:

a reversing downhill around corners

b around corners where the start road is level or slightly uphill as you reverse and changes to sharply downhill as you reverse into the new road

c on corners where there are no kerb stones to help judge the position.

Give a recap of how they have done and praise them for their efforts, even if they have found it difficult. Discuss the session with them by asking them to assess their own performance.

Your examiner

You will be expected to show the ability to control the vehicle accurately whilst reversing to the left. You need to make sure you take the correct observation before, after and during the reverse, whilst showing consideration to other road users.

41 Sweeping left reverse

HIGHWAY CODE
200–203, 206, 263

No two corners are the same and you need to know how to reverse into all types of turning. If the road you are reversing into has a gentle, sweeping curve, you won't need to steer so hard. You will normally be able to keep sight of the corner throughout the manoeuvre.

The principles of reversing are the same as given in the previous session.

Your instructor

Your instructor will discuss your progress and talk you through what you need to practise throughout the lesson. You will be given the opportunity to practise a sweeping reverse as well as uphill and downhill turnings.

You will learn about co-ordination of the controls and steering, observation, speed and the potential risks.

At the end of the lesson your instructor will recap on what you have covered to make sure you have understood everything and explain what the plan is for the next lesson. Your Track Record can be completed accordingly.

Accompanying driver

Explain what is to be practised and take a few moments to discuss what your learner has been taught by their instructor. Check out their Track Record which will show you how they are developing this skill.

Give your learner the opportunity to practise all types of turns. This will allow them to gain the skill of reversing without using a 'method' that only works on right-angled turnings.

Find a quiet junction where the roads are level, with no parked cars in the vicinity of the corner around which the learner will practise reversing. The corner should be sweeping and perhaps have no kerbstones.

Stop in the major road before the corner around which the learner is going to reverse. This allows them to assess the corner and then to drive past it and stop in a suitable position to start the practice. Make sure you:

❑ check their knowledge and understanding of the skill

❑ avoid corners where a tree or post-box is near the kerb or obstructs their view

❑ avoid any road junctions where children are playing

❑ personally check that it is safe just before the car starts to reverse

❑ keep checking all around as the car starts to move

❑ check particularly for oncoming traffic as the learner begins to steer, as the front of the car will swing out.

Make sure your learner:

❑ positions safely and suitably in order to commence the reverse

❑ looks into the turning for any problems

❑ prepares to reverse correctly, including seating position and grip on steering wheel

❑ looks all around before the car moves

❑ looks back over left shoulder while reversing in a straight line towards the corner with frequent glances to the front

❑ checks all round before steering and especially over right shoulder before the front of the car

❑ gives way to other traffic or pedestrians as necessary.

Advanced exercises

Practise:

a reversing downhill around corners

b around corners where the start road is level or slightly uphill as you reverse and changes to sharply downhill as you reverse into the new road

c on corners where there are no kerbstones to help judge the position.

Give a recap of how they have done and praise them for their efforts, even if they have found it difficult. Discuss the session with them by asking them to assess their own performance.

Your examiner

You will be expected to show the ability to control the vehicle accurately while reversing to the left. You need to make sure you take the correct observation before, after and during the reverse, while showing consideration to other road users.

42 Reverse to the right

HIGHWAY CODE
200–203, 206, 263

There are important differences between the right and the left reverse. These differences are to do with your observations.

With the right reverse, you are reversing with the flow of traffic. This means that you need to make frequent forward checks and be prepared to give way to any traffic on your side of the road.

■ As you start to reverse, make sure no traffic is trying to overtake you (A) as your left front wing will swing out (B) – give way to them if necessary. Make sure any vehicle wanting to turn into the road you are reversing into has seen you (C), and that you have spotted any pedestrians wanting to cross the road (D) or children playing nearby (E). Continue reversing well along the new road until there is sufficient room to pull forward onto the other side of the road (F), ready to turn back into the main road when it's safe to do so (G).

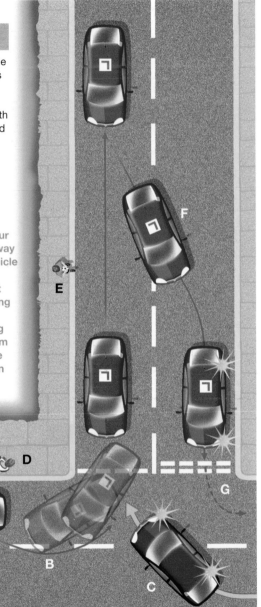

As you reverse around the corner and are about to disappear from the view of any vehicles on the major road, you need to pause and look. If a vehicle wishes to enter the road into which you are reversing, they will of course be driving directly into your path. Make sure that they have seen you. Then continue reversing a short way so that the driver can turn safely without cutting the corner.

Once you are in the new road and have straightened up the wheels, you need to reverse approximately twice as far as you did on the left reverse. This gives you plenty of room to move away and position yourself on the left-hand side of the road again, ready to emerge. Remember that, because you are moving away from the right-hand side of the road, you need to check your left blind spot this time.

You may find it easier if you think about this in four parts:

1. Taking up your position

Pull up on the left-hand side of the road just before the junction on the right around which you are going to reverse. As you move away, take up a position in the road as close to the left of the centre as is safe, as though you were going to do a right turn, but do not give a right-hand signal at this stage.

As you pass the junction on the right, have a look into it to see whether it is safe, legal and convenient to carry out the manoeuvre. Give a right-hand signal if necessary and, once the road is clear, move over to the right-hand side of the road and stop the car about three car lengths from the junction, parallel to and about 40 centimetres (16 inches) from the kerb.

2. To the point of turn

Reverse in a straight line until you get to the point of turn. While doing this, ensure that you move the car slowly, giving yourself time to look properly over both shoulders as

appropriate to the circumstances. While it is important to look over your left shoulder to achieve the best view of the road behind, you must also look over your right shoulder. The advantage of this is that it will help you ensure that your road position near to the kerb is correct. It will also allow you to see into the road that you are about to enter.

As the corner disappears from view through the rear windscreen, switch to your right shoulder. This means you can now see the kerb and judge how little or how much you need to turn the wheel in order to steer the car around the corner.

3. Point of turn

Keep checking all around the vehicle before you begin to steer. Start to steer as soon as you can judge that the rear offside wheel is at the start of the corner.

As the car comes round the corner, straighten the wheels. Keep the car moving slowly and observe all around by checking over both your left and right shoulder as appropriate.

Checking over the left shoulder will allow you to see the road to the rear. Checking over the right shoulder will allow you to see the kerb and the road you are reversing into.

4. Reverse into the new road

Pause to see and be seen before you disappear into the junction, and then continue reversing slowly in a straight line until you are well clear of the junction, about six car lengths. If there are hazard road markings, you could reverse until you were clear of them.

Your instructor

Your instructor will discuss your progress and talk you through what you need to practise throughout the lesson. You will be given the opportunity to practise a reverse to the right, as the observations and positioning are quite different to reversing to the left. You will learn about co-ordination of the controls and steering, observation, speed and the potential risks.

At the end of the lesson your instructor will recap on what you have covered to make sure you have understood everything and explain what the plan is for the next lesson. Your Track Record can be completed accordingly.

Accompanying driver

Explain what is to be practised and take a few moments to discuss what your learner has been taught by their instructor. It is recommended that the learner does not attempt this practice until they can reverse to the left with confidence. Check out their Track Record which will show you how they are developing this skill.

Find a quiet junction where the roads are level, with no parked cars in the vicinity of the corner around which the learner will practise reversing. The corner should be reasonably sharp – nearly a right angle.

Make sure you:

- ☐ check their knowledge and understanding of the skill

- ☐ avoid corners where a tree or post-box is near the kerb or obstructs vision

- ☐ avoid any road where children are playing

- ☐ personally check that it is safe just before the car starts to reverse

- ☐ keep checking all around as the car starts to move

- ☐ check particularly for oncoming traffic as the learner begins to steer since the front of the car will swing out

- ☐ remember that you are actually reversing on the wrong side of the road in the path of oncoming traffic; frequent forward checks are needed; once round the corner, always reverse back until you are well clear of the junction – about six car lengths.

Make sure your learner:

- ☐ positions safely and suitably in order to commence the reverse

- ☐ looks into the turning for any problems

- ☐ prepares to reverse correctly, including their seating position and grip on the steering wheel

- ☐ looks all around before the car moves

- ☐ looks over their right shoulder when reversing to the corner with frequent glances to the front

- ☐ checks all around before steering

- ☐ keeps reasonably close to the kerb

- ☐ looks over their right shoulder, having rounded the corner with frequent glances to the front

- ☐ uses clutch to control speed throughout the exercise unless going downhill

- ☐ continues to reverse in a straight line for a reasonable distance and stops safely well back from the junction

❏ gives way to other traffic or pedestrians as necessary.

Advanced exercises

Practise:

a on corners which are long, gentle curves, not right-angles

b reversing uphill around corners

c reversing downhill around corners

d around corners where the start road is level or slightly uphill as you reverse and changes to sharply downhill as you reverse into the new road

e on corners where there are no kerbstones to help judge the position.

Give a recap of how they have done and praise them for their efforts, even if they have found it difficult. Discuss the session with them by asking them to assess their own performance.

Your examiner

You will be expected to show the ability to control the vehicle accurately while reversing to the right. You need to make sure you take the correct observation before, after and during the reverse, whilst showing consideration to other road users.

43 Turn in the road

**HIGHWAY CODE
200, 202**

If there are no side roads or openings to reverse into, and the road is not wide enough to allow you to make a U-turn, you will need to turn your car around by a series of forward and backward movements. This is often called a three-point turn although the number of movements needed to complete the turn will depend on the width of the road, the length of your car, its steering lock and your ability to handle the controls.

The skills involved are also very useful for getting yourself out of a tight parking position. You may need to move the car forwards and backwards, steering to full lock and back again several times before you can move away.

The minimum number of moves you can make for a turn in the road is three, so let's look at how you would put this into practice, referring to the diagram on the following page.

You may find it easier to think about it in three moves:

1. Move off and steer forward

The first of the three moves involves taking the car from a parked position on the left-hand side of the road and steering it across the road, ideally aiming for a 90° angle to the kerb. You must wait to steer until the car is moving and then get full right lock on in the shortest possible distance. Keep that lock on for as long as you dare, leaving yourself enough time and room to steer the wheels back to the left without hitting the kerb.

You need to steer the wheels back to the left because, when you start reversing in the second part of the manoeuvre, the back end of the car needs to move to the left first. If you stop with the wheels still on full right lock,

131

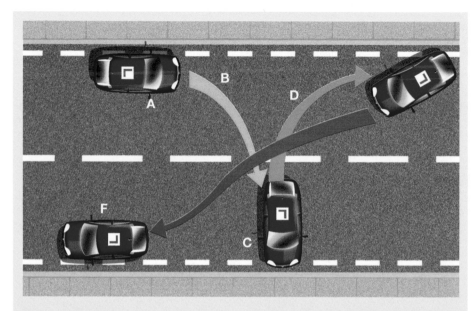

Use clutch control to creep slowly forwards (A), turning the wheel quickly and fully to the right. Keep looking all around (B).

When the front of the car is about a metre from the kerb, steer quickly to the left, braking to a stop before the front wheels touch the kerb (C). Look at the camber of the road. The curve in the road surface may cause the car to speed up.

Put on the hand brake, and prepare to reverse. Use clutch control to hold the car still, and look all around before moving backwards.

Use clutch control to creep slowly backwards (D), steering quickly to the left. Keep looking all around, particularly over your right shoulder. The right side of the car will reach the kerb first.

When the back of the car is about a metre from the kerb, steer quickly to the right. Brake to a stop just before the boot of the car overhangs the kerb, and before the rear wheels touch the kerb (E).

Put on the hand brake and prepare to move the car forwards. Look all around before moving. Drive slowly forwards, steering as necessary to reach the left-hand side of the road (F). Park on the left, and put your seatbelt back on.

when you start reversing the car will move in the direction from which it has just come and you risk not completing the manoeuvre. It is only necessary to straighten the wheels or get them turned just slightly to the left.

Have a good look all around the car before you start moving and do not move if you see a vehicle coming towards you from either direction; let them go first. Look out for pedestrians and wait if they are passing.

Once you start the manoeuvre, look mainly right as you steer right, and left as you steer left. This keeps you focusing in the direction from which your immediate danger is coming.

Keep the car moving reasonably slowly, using clutch control. Take care as the car comes over the crown of the road as, depending on the severity of the camber, you may need to switch to brake control to prevent the car rolling away from you. Stop before you touch the kerb and apply the parking brake.

2. Move off and steer reverse

Select reverse gear and get the car ready for an uphill start. Have a good look all around, especially over both shoulders through the rear windscreen and at the pavement towards which you will be reversing. Give way to any pedestrians.

As you start to move, steer quickly and fully to the left. Keep observing over your left shoulder through the rear windscreen and, as you cross the crown of the road, switch your observations to over your right shoulder. Your immediate danger would now be coming from the right. Also, you can judge the proximity of the kerb better because the offside rear wheel is closest to it.

About a metre from the kerb, start steering to the right and stop the car just before you get to the kerb. Again, when taking the lock off, it is only necessary to straighten the wheels or

get them turned just slightly to the right so that when you move away the car will head off to the right. Stop before you touch the kerb and apply the parking brake if the camber requires it.

3. Moving off and steering forward

Select first gear and, if there is a camber, prepare for an uphill start. Have a good look all around and give way to any other road users. When it is safe, move off slowly, steering to the right.

It is at this point that you can decide whether in fact you can complete the manoeuvre in three turns or whether you need five. If you think you are going to mount the kerb, steer the wheels to the left as you get closer to the kerb and stop. You will need to repeat parts two and three of the manoeuvre.

Observation

Problems can arise when another vehicle appears on the scene while you are in the middle of carrying out this manoeuvre. Usually, it is best to complete the part of the turn you are doing. The other driver has far more chance of being able to steer around you than if you had stopped in the middle of the road.

Your best bet is to look at the other driver to see what they intend doing. Allow them to make up their own mind about whether they wish to drive past you or whether they are going to wait and let you complete the manoeuvre.

Don't beckon them through, as you may be putting them at unnecessary risk if you haven't noticed something coming from the other direction. If the other driver is obviously going to wait for you, don't hang about, but also don't panic. There is a temptation to rush because someone is waiting – don't give in to it. Rushing easily causes mistakes.

Your instructor

Your instructor will discuss your progress and talk you through what you need to practise throughout the lesson.

You will begin by practising on very quiet roads and progress to roads where other traffic is likely to appear. In that way you get used to coping with the pressure of the situation. It is a good idea to try out this exercise when facing both up and down fairly steep hills so that you get used to the different moments when you will need clutch or brake control.

At the end of the lesson your instructor will recap on what you have covered to make sure you have understood everything and explain what the plan is for the next lesson. Your Track Record can be completed accordingly.

Accompanying driver

Explain what is to be practised and take a few moments to discuss what your learner has been taught by their instructor. Check out their Track Record which will show you how they are developing this skill.

Find a quiet and fairly wide, level road, preferably with a reasonably gentle camber. Park on the left, well away from parked cars on either side of the road and any trees or other obstacles close to the kerb.

Make sure you:

❑ check their knowledge and understanding of the skill

❑ avoid conducting this practise where a tree or post-box is near the kerb and would be immediately in front or behind as you drive across the road and reverse back

❑ avoid any road where children are playing

❑ personally check that it is safe throughout the manoeuvre

❑ check particularly for other traffic, and, when necessary, advise the learner to give way

❑ do not let the learner drive or reverse towards pedestrians on the pavement

❑ if other traffic waves at the learner to continue, be sure they really mean it

❑ are aware that another car waiting puts pressure on the learner and may cause them to stall.

Make sure your learner:

❑ parks safely and suitably in order to commence the manoeuvre

❑ looks all around before the car moves

❑ waits for any traffic to pass

❑ looks in appropriate directions to check it's safe throughout the manoeuvre

❑ controls the speed

❑ steers briskly and steers back at the appropriate time

❑ applies the parking brake when stopped at the end of each phase of the manoeuvre

- ❏ maintains control and does not roll forwards or back on the camber

- ❏ avoids touching the kerb

- ❏ parks safely at the end of the manoeuvre.

Advanced exercises

Practise on:

a increasingly narrow roads

b where some other traffic is likely to pass during the manoeuvre

c hills facing up at the start of the manoeuvre

d hills facing down at the start of the manoeuvre

e roads with a steep camber.

Give a recap of how they have done and praise them for their efforts, even if they have found it difficult. Discuss the session with them by asking them to assess their own performance.

Your examiner

Your examiner will ask you to stop at a convenient place and ask you to turn the car around. You are expected to complete the exercise in as few moves as possible, without touching the kerb.

You must show you are in full control of the car. Keep looking all around and be careful not to cause any danger to other traffic or pedestrians. Try not to cause unnecessary delay to any waiting vehicles.

44 Reverse park

HIGHWAY CODE
200, 202, 239–252

Imagine that you are driving through a busy high street shopping area. You need to park your car and there is a line of cars already parked along the road. There is also a lot of moving traffic behind and ahead of you. You are travelling slowly, looking for a space, and you think you can see one. You now check behind to see how close the following traffic is.

You indicate to the left and you gently brake so as to pull up just before the gap. This now gives you the chance to assess the suitability of the gap. You need to decide whether it is:

Safe
Is it on a bend or near the brow of a hill or too close to a junction? Is there any broken glass in the gutter? Are there any pedestrians using the gap to cross the road? Are there any children playing?

Convenient
Is there a driveway in the gap, or might somebody need access to the entrance or to a garage? Are you going to narrow the road too much by carrying out a reverse park?

Legal
Do parking restrictions prevent you from parking there at all, or are you limited to a certain amount of time?

Suitable
You should consider any gradient and the necessary techniques to control the speed. You also need to consider the camber, because if it is steep you will have to use the brake for control.

You need a minimum space of one-and-a-half times the length of your own vehicle in order to be able to manoeuvre your car into the gap,

135

1. The parking gap should be at least one-and-a-half car lengths.

2. Stop parallel to the front parked car, about one metre away.

3. Reverse until the backs of the cars are level and turn the wheel one-and-a-half times to the left. Remember that the car front will swing out as you move.

4. As you see the door mirror of your car line up with the back of the other car, turn the steering wheel one-and-a-half times to the right.

5. When you see the offside corner of the other car in the bottom-left corner of your windscreen, steer one-and-a-half times to the right.

6. When you are almost parallel with the kerb steer one-and-a-half times to the left to straighten the wheels and stop.

7. If necessary, move backwards or forwards to straighten up.

about a space of at least twice the length of your vehicle. You need to think quickly and act with confidence.

When parking, check your mirrors and slowly pull forwards. If you pull up immediately in front of the gap, ready to reverse into it, you may find that the following vehicle has pulled up right behind you, preventing you from reversing into your selected space. If you pull up before the gap you have a better chance of assessing it and of allowing other road users to understand your intentions.

You may need to indicate to the left again as

you stop ahead of the gap. Your brake lights act as a signal to inform other road users that you are not moving off.

Select reverse gear as soon as you can. This is also a useful signal and, in selecting reverse, you can cancel your indicator. Now you are ready to reverse into the gap. The speed of your car matched to the speed at which you turn the wheel, where and when you look, and your accuracy, are all crucial to how successful you are in parking your car first time. So don't dawdle, but do take your time and, within reason, don't worry about holding up the other traffic.

■ It's important to remember that in the test there may not actually be a car defining the rear of the space, in which case you must use your imagination.

Take care over when and where you look. Bear in mind that pedestrians often cross the road in gaps; children can break free from adults and run into the road; dogs can also run out. Vehicles coming up behind you may choose to steer around you, and in doing so may need to move into the path of oncoming traffic, so be prepared to give way.

The front end of the car will swing out, narrowing the width of the road even more. Look mainly over your left shoulder through the rear windscreen, which is the direction in which the car is moving.

Your instructor

Your instructor will discuss your progress and talk you through what you need to practise throughout the lesson. In the beginning your instructor will choose a very quiet road, with a large gap between the cars. As you will be taking a little longer to complete the exercise this will not inconvenience other drivers. As your skills improve, you can progress to smaller gaps and busier roads.

At the end of the lesson your instructor will recap on what you have covered to make sure you have understood everything, and explain what the plan is for the next lesson. Your Track Record can be completed accordingly.

Accompanying driver

Explain what is to be practised and take a few moments to discuss what your learner has been taught by their instructor. Early stages of practice are best left to the instructor who has the advantage of the dual controls. Check out their Track Record which will show you how they are developing this skill.

Find a quiet, level road with a parked car which has a long gap behind it of at least three car lengths or no other car at all. Stop and park further back down the road in a position from which both you and the learner can see the gap into which you intend the learner to reverse.

Make sure you:

❏ check their knowledge and understanding of the skill

❏ give your learner a chance to study the gap by stopping further back down the road

❏ keep a continuous lookout for other vehicles and pedestrians

❏ make sure you are not too near a bend or the brow of a hill

❏ avoid roads where children are playing

❏ avoid a place that would block someone's driveway or narrow the road too much

❏ are sure that it is legal to park there

❏ avoid hills or steeply cambered roads for first attempts at this exercise

❏ stop the practice and start again if things begin to go terribly wrong

❏ don't allow the learner to get too close to any other vehicles.

Make sure your learner:

❏ warns other drivers of the intention, by giving an early signal if necessary

❏ positions safely and suitably in order to commence the reverse

❏ prepares to reverse correctly, including seating position and grip on steering wheel

❏ looks all around before the car moves

❏ looks mainly over left shoulder when reversing, with frequent glances all around

❏ checks all around before steering left, which brings the rear end of the car in, but swings the front end out into the road

❏ reverses slowly under clutch control

❏ does not steer too much or too little

❏ does not hit the kerb

❏ stops parallel to the kerb and reasonably close to it.

Advanced exercises

Practise:

a on busier roads

b reversing into a smaller gap, but never less than one-and-a-half car lengths

c on hills both up and down

d on a road with a very steep camber

e reversing into a gap on the right-hand side of the road; either choose a very quiet road or a quiet one-way street.

Give a recap of how they have done and praise them for their efforts, even if they have found it difficult. Discuss the session with them by asking them to assess their own performance.

45 Reversing into a bay

HIGHWAY CODE
239

45 Reversing into a bay

Your examiner

You will be expected to control the vehicle accurately and take full and effective observations throughout the manoeuvre. You should also consider other traffic and complete the exercise without undue hesitation.

This is a life skill that you will use time and time again. Drive your car forward level with the bay into which you want to park and then, depending on space, draw forward at an angle to either right or left so that the back of your vehicle is pointing towards the bay which you want to use. Make sure that you check it is safe before swinging to either right or left.

Reverse into the bay and try to finish up within the white lines and with the whole of the car within the box.

While reversing it is acceptable to have a quick glance out of the offside window but you must not hang your head out of this side and neglect all-round observation.

The secret of success in this exercise is to keep the car under control, moving slowly, and keep looking all around the vehicle.

Your instructor

Your instructor will discuss your progress and talk you through what you need to practise throughout the lesson. You will be given the opportunity to practise this exercise, either in a car park or at quiet times in the test centre car park itself. At the very least your instructor will show you the parking bays at the centre so you know what to expect on the day.

At the end of the lesson your instructor will recap on what you have covered to make sure you have understood everything and explain what the plan is for the next lesson. Your Track Record can be completed accordingly.

■ When reversing into a parking space, the same position in your seat and your grip on the steering wheel are the same as for reversing in a straight line (exercise 39).

Accompanying driver

Find a car park where at least one section is reasonably quiet and which has clearly marked parking bays. Initially you may find it less stressful to choose a bay for the learner to park in with another car on one side only and without another occupied bay or a brick wall immediately behind it. Make sure you:

❑ check their knowledge and understanding of the skill

❑ keep a continuous lookout for other vehicles and pedestrians

❑ stop the exercise and start again if things start to go terribly wrong

❑ do not allow the learner to get too close to any other vehicles.

Make sure your learner:

❑ positions safely and suitably in order to commence the reverse

❑ prepares to reverse correctly, including seating position and grip on steering wheel

❑ looks all around before the car moves

❑ looks mainly over left shoulder when reversing, with frequent glances all around

❑ checks all around before steering and swinging to left or right

❑ reverses slowly under clutch control

❑ does not steer too much or too little

❑ stops within the parking bay

❑ stops parallel to the white lines and a reasonable distance from any car to either side

❑ stops before any obstruction to the rear of the vehicle

❑ does not protrude unnecessarily from the front of the parking bay.

Advanced exercises

Practise:

a in a busier car park

b with an obstruction behind the parking bay and cars parked on both sides

c where limited space makes it difficult to find a position from which to reverse easily.

d in a car park where the bays are narrower than normal

e reversing into a parking bay from the right.

Reversing into a bay to park is eco-friendly because moving off forwards uses less fuel than in reverse. It also gives you far better visibility around the car.

Give a recap of how they have done and praise them for their efforts, even if they have found it difficult. Discuss the session with them by asking them to assess their own performance.

Your examiner

You should show that you can reverse into a bay, with effective all-round observation, and consideration of others. You should be able to control your car so that you reverse neatly and stop within the marked bay without excessive repositioning.

■ For a first session, try to find a spot in the car park where there are two or more free bays for the learner to reverse into.

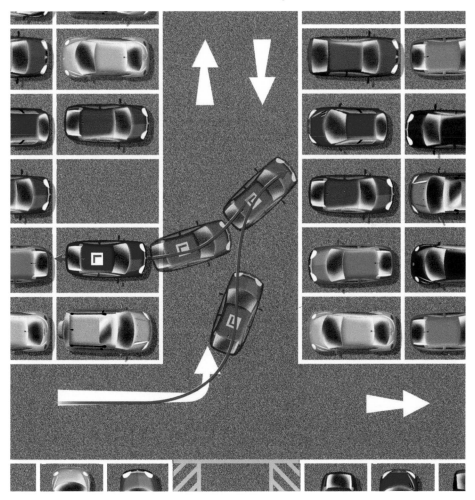

Section 5
The Driving Test

Are you really ready? Remember
your goal of passing first time? It
would be a shame to take the test
too early and have to go through the
time and expense of taking it again.

■ An early start...

Your Track Record

Your Completed Track Record

You will not be ready for your test until you have completed your Track Record to level 5 on each of the 45 skills.

Mock test

Once you have completed the Track Record, your instructor wll arrange for you to have a Mock Test. This will allow you to experience a test route while driving completely unprompted. Your instructor will discuss how you did and advise on whether you are ready for the test. Remember that skill levels can dip.

Accompanying driver

It's best to abide by the instructor's advice as to whether the learner is ready to take the test. The instructor wants to see a pass, not only for personal pride but also so that the learner will develop into a safe driver for life. If you're supporting the learner financially as well as practically, any delay can be frustrating if you feel your learner is ready, but taking the test too soon can be a false economy.

Booking the test

Because some test centres have longer waiting lists than others, take advice from your instructor who is in a better position to judge the right time to apply.

You need to have taken and passed the Theory Test within the last two years.

An instructor can book your test for you, or you can go online at: www.direct.gov.uk.

At the Driving Test Centre

It's normal to feel nervous, but try not to be. If you drive like you do on your lessons then you should pass. Your examiner will not take you into situations where you can't cope and will try to put you at your ease.

Arrive in plenty of time. If you arrive late, you may not be able to take the test.

Make sure you have originals of:

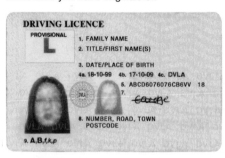

❏ both parts of your photo licence

❏ your Theory Test certificate

❏ your booking number.

If you are not taking the test in your instructor's car, make sure your vehicle is:

❏ taxed with a certificate displayed

❏ showing L-plates (D-Plates in Wales) to the front and rear, not obscuring the view

❏ in a roadworthy condition and has an MOT certificate (if required)

VT20	MOT Test Certificate	VOSA

This certificate has been issued according to the conditions and notes on the back of this certificate. Vehicle & Operator Services Agency

Note: if you have doubts as to whether this certificate is valid, please use the service described in note 3 overleaf to check.

MOT test number	Make	Odometer reading
270339066231	HONDA	60060 Miles
Registration mark	Model	Test class
XV26XSS	CIVIC	IV
Vehicle identification or chassis number	Colour	Approximate year of first use
ZNME387468U008265	SILVER	2001
Expiry date	Issue date/time	Fuel type
SEPTEMBER 25th 2007 (ZERO SEVEN)	SEPTEMBER 26th 2006 (ZERO SIX) 16:57	Petrol
Authorisation number		Design gross weight (goods vehicles)	kg
		Advisory Notice issued	NO
		Test station number	009660

❏ legal – that is, all the lights are working, it has the required number of mirrors (nearside and offside from 1978), the speedometer is working and shows both mph and km/h

❏ fully covered by insurance for you to drive

❏ fitted with head restraints (not slip-on type)

❏ fitted with fully functional seat belts

❏ fitted with an interior rear-view mirror for the examiner to use.

Some convertible vehicles are unsuitable for the driving test due to the lack of all-round vision for the examiner. If you propose to use a convertible vehicle for the driving test, please check its suitability when you book.

You can't take your test if your vehicle:

❏ does not have a seat for the examiner

❏ has no clear view to the rear, other than by means of the mirrors

❏ is over 3.5 tonnes in weight

❏ is loaded or partly loaded

❏ is towing a trailer

❏ has more than eight passenger seats.

Some cars have been subjected to a manufacturer's recall. You will need to bring a certificate to prove you have had the work carried out.

At the time of your appointment, your examiner will enter the waiting room and call your name. You will then be asked to sign an identity and insurance check and produce your licence. Once that is done you make your way to the car park.

145

After an introduction the examiner will try to put you at ease. Examiners have no fixed quotas for passes and fails and want all their candidates to do well, whatever horror stories you may have heard. If you drive as you and your instructor know you can, you should pass.

Just the two of us?
On some occasions a supervising officer might accompany the examiner and will sit in the back of the car. Don't worry, they are not testing you, but ensuring that testing standards are consistent. They won't interfere with the test at all.

Your instructor can accompany you on your test, seated in the back of the car. It is up to you: some people prefer it and some feel

■ The examiner will try to put you at ease before the test begins.

easier on their own with the examiner. In any case, at the end of the test you should call your instructor over to listen to the examiner's debriefing.

Stay calm
Taking any kind of test is likely to make you feel that you've got butterflies in your stomach. You need to get them to fly in formation by knowing what to expect.

Some nervousness is normal when taking any examination, and they actually can improve your performance.

The secret to success depends on two things. The first is being fully prepared by knowing what to expect and the second is to think positively by believing in yourself.

So be sure you've completed and practised the whole syllabus before taking the test – don't put too much pressure on yourself – the world won't end if you fail. Not telling your friends when your test is can help keep the pressure off.

Keep practising what your instructor has taught you 'in your head'. It is possible to improve your ability to perform co-ordinated tasks by imagining that you're doing them.

Get a good night's sleep before the test. Have all your ID documents ready so that you're not looking for them in the morning! As soon as you wake up on the morning of your test, tell yourself that you are going to get through the day calmly.

If you find yourself making 'out of character' mistakes on the drive before the test, don't worry. This isn't unusual.

It's a good idea to arrive at the Driving Test Centre early so that you don't feel rushed. The time allowed for the whole test, including the formalities at the beginning and the end, is almost an hour.

Just before you meet the examiner, relax by taking a few slow deep breaths. Clenching and then relaxing your muscles can relieve tension.

If you want your instructor to sit in the back during the test, that's not a problem. Just ask the examiner at the start.

From the point you meet the examiner, listen carefully to the directions and ask for them to be repeated if you are unsure. Follow the road ahead unless traffic signs or the examiner

direct you otherwise. Forget it's an examiner sitting next to you – imagine it's your silent instructor sat by your side!

Don't panic if you come across a tricky or new situation. Keep looking well ahead, read the circumstances and use the driving plan – Mirrors – Signal – Manoeuvre (MSM), to help decide on the best action to take.

When you return to the Driving Test Centre your examiner will ask you to park and then tell you the result.

Eyesight test

You will be asked to read a number plate at a set distance. If you have a little trouble with it your examiner will take you a little nearer. If you still have trouble, you will be asked to return to the waiting room while the distance is measured (from another vehicle). If you cannot read it this time, you will fail the test.

Show me, tell me

Your examiner will ask you two questions regarding vehicle safety. One requires you to show how you would carry out the checks. They will be chosen from the following:

❑ **Show me / explain how you would check that the power-assisted steering is working before starting a journey.**

If the steering becomes heavy, the system may not be working properly. Before starting a journey, two simple checks can be made. Gentle pressure on the steering wheel, maintained while the engine is started, should result in a slight but noticeable movement as the system begins to operate. Turning the steering wheel just after moving off will give an immediate indication that the power assistance is working.

❑ **Open the bonnet, identify where you would check the engine oil level and tell**

me how you would check that the engine has sufficient oil.

You should identify the dipstick/oil level indicator and describe the oil level against the minimum/maximum markers.

❏ **Identify where the windscreen washer reservoir is and tell me how you would check the windscreen washer level.**

You should identify the reservoir and explain how to check the level.

❏ **Show me how you would check that the horn is working (off-road only).**

Check the horn (turn on ignition if necessary).

❏ **Open the bonnet, identify where the brake fluid reservoir is and tell me how you would check that you have a safe level of hydraulic brake fluid.**

You should identify the reservoir, check the level against high/low markings.

❏ **Show me how you would check that the direction indicators are working.**

Apply the indicators or hazard warning switch and check all indicators.

❏ **Tell me how you would check that the brake lights are working on this car.**

Operate brake pedal, make use of reflections in windows, garage doors, etc, or ask someone to help.

❏ **Show me how you would check the parking brake for excessive wear.**

Apply the parking brake so that when it is fully applied it secures itself, and is not at the end of the working travel.

❏ **Tell me how you would check that the brakes are working before starting a journey.**

The brakes should not feel spongy or slack. They should be tested as you set off and the vehicle should not pull to one side.

❑ **Show me how you would check that the headlights and tail lights are working.**

You should operate the switch (turn on ignition if necessary), and walk around the vehicle.

❑ **Tell me where you would find the information for the recommended tyre pressures for this car and how tyre pressures should be checked.**

This is found in the manufacturer's guide. Using a reliable pressure gauge, check and adjust the pressures when the tyres are cold. Don't forget the spare tyre and remember to refit the valve caps.

❑ **Tell me how you would check the tyres to ensure that they have sufficient tread depth and that their general condition is safe to use on the road.**

There must be no cuts and bulges and have at least 1.6mm of tread depth across the central $\frac{3}{4}$ of the breadth of the tyre and around the entire outer circumference.

On the road

Your examiner will give you a quick overview of the test and explain that you will be driving on different types of road, just as you have on your lessons. All the instructions will be given in good time, so relax. If you are not sure of anything, ask.

The examiner is looking for safety, awareness and confidence. You'll be treated as though you are driving unaccompanied, so you won't be prompted on how to act on signals, unexpected conditions or situations.

How you are assessed

Your examiner will watch you as you drive and assess any errors. Those worthy of note will be recorded on the Driving Test Report. Don't worry if you see them do this – it might not be a serious fault, and might not result in failure. The markings have the following criteria:

Driving fault
This is a less serious fault because of the circumstances at the time. If you have 15 of these, you will fail.

Serious fault
Marked as serious because there is a habitual driving fault or a potential dangerous incident.

Dangerous fault
When a fault causes actual danger. The examiner might take action in this case.

If you don't pass

You may have taken your test too soon, or made an error dealing with something you would normally cope with. In either case you have made mistakes that could have caused danger. Listen to the debrief that your examiner gives you as it will help you understand what mistakes you made and how you can improve for next time.

You will be given the Driving Test Report to take away with you. Discuss the marks given with your instructor.

If you pass

Well done – it's a reward for all that hard work. You should look at the Driving Test Report and discuss the marks with your instructor because there is always room for improvement.

Section 6
You've passed!

Congratulations!

Now you have the freedom and independence that having a driving licence brings.

It also brings its own responsibilities, so make sure you have the right attitude.

Having the right attitude

HIGHWAY CODE
90, 91, 95, 147-150, Annexes 5, 8

Yes, you've passed your test, but you need to continue to develop your skills and experiences so you lessen your risk of being involved in a crash. The statistics show that 18 percent of new drivers have a crash in the first year after taking their tests. This is not only as a result of their lack of experience but can be caused by failing to take the correct attitude towards driving.

The risks

Most of the worst collisions and crashes happen between midnight and 6am. The hazards of driving in darkness combined with socialising makes this a high-risk time.

Carrying passengers

If you are carrying passengers, you are responsible for their safety. Are you putting them at risk? You need to concentrate at all times when driving; don't let them distract you. You could risk having a crash if you:

❏ show off, or try to race other drivers

❏ drink or take drugs before driving

❏ drive too fast for the conditions

❏ use a mobile phone when driving

❏ drive while tired.

If your passengers tease you in any way about your attitude, suggest they walk or take public transport.

You should also be aware that the car you learned in is not a high-powered car – before you attempt to drive one you should gain more experience.

■ No matter how tempting it may be, don't let your friends egg you on to drive irresponsibly, and ignore their teasing.

New Drivers Act 1995
There are special rules for new drivers regarding penalty points.

If you receive six penalty points within the first two years of passing your test you will have to give up your licence and start all over again.

Yes, that includes the Theory Test. If you think your insurance is high now, just think what effect losing your licence would have. And think on this: **two speeding offences means six points**.

Electronic Devices

HIGHWAY CODE
149, 150, 270

It is illegal to use a hand-held device while driving (unless in an emergency). This includes:

- ❏ mobile phones

- ❏ MP3 Players

- ❏ navigation systems.

You need to be concentrating on your driving at all times. You should not make this more difficult by carrying on a conversation on the phone or fiddling with controls. It is safer not to use a phone at all, even if it is hands-free. Turn off your phone, and wait until you stop to pick up any messages.

Be aware that changing stations on your radio, or setting a dashboard-placed navigation system, can also distract you.

Accompanying driver

Your learner has passed the test. Congratulations, your hard work has paid off, but really this is where the worrying begins. You know what your driver's weaknesses are and now they are out there on their own. Are you going to lie awake at night waiting for them to come home? Probably.

We know that the high-risk times are after midnight, so it might be prudent to lay some ground rules at the start of the learning process. If you are making a financial commitment to their training and their use

■ Don't let a good time out become a distraction on the drive home – restrict the number of passengers you carry to just one at first.

of a car once qualified then it might be easier than if they are fully independent.

Peer pressure can be very difficult to resist, however well-intentioned it might be.

Come to an arrangement with your driver that they:

❑ complete Pass Plus

❑ restrict the number of passengers to one

❑ don't use their car after 9pm

❑ don't drive if they think they might be in an environment where they could drink alcohol.

■ Driving requires all your attention – don't let anything distract you from it.

Pass Plus

Pass Plus is a programme of six modules, over a minimum of six lessons, specially designed by the Driving Standards Agency (DSA) for the newly qualified driver.

You'll get further expert instruction on specific elements of driving and learn a wider range of skills to better prepare for the conditions you'll face on the road. And there's a good chance you can take the Pass Plus course with your current instructor.

The six Pass Plus modules are:

1. Town driving

2. All-weather driving

3. Out of town driving

4. Night driving

5. Dual carriageways

6. Motorway driving

There's no test – you just reach the required standard in each module and your instructor dates and signs it off.

After you've successfully completed all six modules, the form is sent to the DSA, who will award you with a certificate. As well as helping to make you a safer and more confident driver, Pass Plus could also save you up to 30 percent on your insurance. Come renewal time, just show your certificate to your insurer.

For more information about the Pass Plus scheme, ask your instructor or contact your local BSM centre.

Owning a car

The first thing you need to do is calculate whether you can afford a car of your own. It's not only the purchase price that you need to think about, but also the cost of road tax, insurance, maintenance and fuel to run it. Depreciation – how much it will lose in value while you own it – is also a factor.

Most people do not start their driving career by buying a new car. They're far more likely to buy a second-hand one, and care is needed to ensure that what you buy is a sensible purchase in relation to the price you can afford. Unless you have mechanical knowledge, it is worth paying an expert to assess your intended purchase.

For peace of mind, you can arrange a structural, mechanical and safety aspects examination. This can also include a performance and handling road test. The RAC offers this service, which can save you much worry and helps take the risk out of buying a used vehicle.

As well as thinking about the look and style of the car, when choosing the type and model of car consider:

❏ your seating comfort and headroom

❏ whether the engine size is right for your regular journeys

❏ whether you prefer manual or automatic gears

❏ its capacity and how many passengers or equipment you might need to carry

❏ its resale value

❏ if it will fit in your driveway, car port or garage.

Test drive the types of car you like before making your choice. Always shop around and check out deals on the Internet. Don't rush into a decision and never be afraid of asking for a discount.

It is wise to check the car's finance history, specifically for any outstanding hire purchase. It is also possible to check whether the vehicle has ever been written off or stolen.

Read your car handbook and stick to the manufacturer's recommendations. Have your car serviced at regular intervals - it will use less fuel - and keep a record of any work done as this will help when selling the car on.

For your own safety ensure that your car is always in a good roadworthy condition. You can reduce the risk of breakdown by carrying out your daily and weekly checks. When you do your daily checks, walk around your car and look for obvious problems such as flat tyres, damage to lights and loose trim.

Remember the car safety checks you learned for your test and put them into practice.

Membership of a breakdown organisation, such as the RAC, will take away much of your worry and stress.

For your information, contact RAC on:
0800 029 029 **or visit:** www.rac.co.uk

Section 7
Motorways

HIGHWAY CODE
253-273, 274-277, 290

You will have prepared for your test by driving on faster dual carriageways, but as it is against the law, you will not have been given the opportunity to use the motorway.

Getting ready

Motorways can have as many as six lanes, so it is a good idea to be accompanied when you make your first journey on one. Make sure you:

- check your vehicle is legal and in good working order. Carry out your POWER checks (see pages 21–23)

- have read and understood rules 253-290 of The Highway Code

- are aware of the warning signs and signals

- are fit and not feeling tired

- plan your route in advance – you must not park anywhere on the motorway except at a service area (except in an emergency)

- plan a stop for every two hours of driving (if you are using a map, look at alternative routes in case there are problems on the motorway). You can plan a route at www.rac.co.uk

- set the satellite navigation system, if you have one

- check the weather and traffic conditions at www.rac.co.uk

- are prepared for and know the procedures if you breakdown. For information about the RAC breakdown service check online at www.rac.co.uk

- turn off your phone.

Joining a motorway

You will normally join the motor via a slip road. Make sure you:

- assess the speed of the traffic already on the motorway and adjust your speed

- use the MSPSL routine (a quick sideways glance will help) and join where there is a suitable gap in the traffic

■ Stay in your lane when you encounter 'splitter lanes'.

- give priority to the traffic already on the motorway

- don't assume other drivers will slow down or change lanes to let you onto the motorway

- don't cause drivers on the motorway to brake harshly or change lanes dangerously

- don't drive along the hard shoulder (unless permitted by signage).

Motorway driving

Once you are on the motorway, keep to the left lane while you get used to the speed of the traffic. Make sure you:

- cancel your signal

- keep your eyes moving all around

- make frequent mirror checks

- keep up with the speed of the traffic

- use the two-second rule (4 seconds in wet conditions and up to 10 in ice or snow)

- keep within your lane unless you are overtaking or responding to direction signs

- use the MSM routine in good time.

Overtaking
If you are gaining on the car in front and wish to overtake, do so only on the right-hand side.

Make sure you:

- check all around (mirrors and a sideways glance)

- check there is enough room in the lane to your right

- signal

- move out without steering harshly

- don't cut in on the vehicle you have overtaken if you are moving back into the left lane; other drivers need their separation distance too.

When the motorway is busy the traffic stream in the left lane might be moving quicker than that on the right. In this case you should keep up with the flow of traffic even if it means passing the traffic on your right.

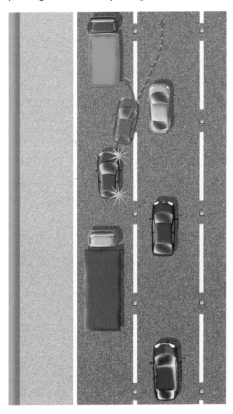

■ Try to avoid getting 'boxed in' by other vehicles and prevented from overtaking.

159

Dealing with large vehicles

Large vehicles are involved in a large proportion of crashes on our motorways. You need to be aware of the dangers when dealing with them.

Always keep your separation distance. This does three things:

❑ gives you a safe stopping distance

❑ allows you see more of the road ahead, instead of just the rear of the large vehicle in front

❑ allows the driver of the large vehicle to see you in the mirrors.

When overtaking a large vehicle make sure you:

❑ use your safety routine

❑ try to overtake without getting yourself 'sandwiched'. Try to time it so that you have a clear lane on your right – this will give you a safety margin if the large vehicle moves out of their lane

Motorway lane discipline

Hard shoulder
For emergency use only, unless otherwise allowed in those areas under Active Traffic Management (ATM).

Left-hand lane
Use this lane unless overtaking.

In an emergency it is much easier to reach the hard shoulder if you are driving next to it.

Do not straddle lanes

Middle lane
Use this lane to overtake traffic in the left-hand lane.

You may stay in the middle lane if you are overtaking a line of slower-moving vehicles. This is safer than moving in and out repeatedly.

Right-hand lane
Use this lane to overtake traffic in the middle lane.

Large Goods Vehicles (LGVs) – vehicles towing trailers and passenger vehicles with maximum laden weight exceeding 7.5 tonnes constructed or adapted to carry more than eight seated passengers in addition to the driver – are not allowed to use this lane if all three lanes are open.

The illuminated signals on the central reservation or at the back of the hard shoulder apply to all lanes of the motorway.

- are aware that the vehicle might be a left-hand drive and therefore have blind spots along the right-hand side of the vehicle

- switch on your wipers to fast speed well before you overtake in wet weather - the spray from the wheels can badly affect your visibility.

The hard shoulder

Unless it is being used as part of an Active Traffic Management (ATM) system, the hard shoulder should only be used in an emergency. Do not use it for:

- resting

- changing drivers

- checking maps

- answering the phone

Saving fuel

Driving on motorways can be more economical with fuel than driving across country. To ensure you achieve the best economies make sure you look and plan well ahead. This will allow you to:

- plan any overtaking in good time, without losing your separation distance

- prevent using the brake harshly, when taking your foot off the accelerator will allow you to slow down gradually.

Use cruise control if fitted, and be aware that reducing your cruising speed will make a big difference to the amount of fuel you use.

Leaving the motorway

All exits on the motorway are numbered so if you have planned your route you will know when the exit you want is coming up.

Make sure you:

- look out for signs showing your exit

- get into the correct lane in good time

- don't leave it too late or cut across several lanes at once

- adjust your speed on the exit slip road as this is likely to lead to a junction

- are aware that you may have to get used to the slower-moving traffic on the next road you join; keep checking your speed.

161

Your instructor

Your instructor can arrange for you to take a motorway driving simulator programme. The two-hour programme is designed to provide new drivers with a realistic introduction to motorway driving.

It allows you to practise joining the motorway, keeping the right distance away from other traffic, overtaking and leaving the motorway. You also have the chance to drive in rain and fog as well as negotiating motorway road works and driving at night time.

You are strongly advised to take part in Pass Plus which includes a motorway session. Pass Plus must be a minimum of six hours training, but this can be extended if you require further instruction in any of the modules, including motorway driving.

Accompanying driver

It is advised that your learner take their Pass Plus instruction before you accompany them on the motorway.

Make sure you:

❑ check their knowledge and understanding of motorway driving

❑ plan the route with your learner before leaving

❑ introduce your learner to a motorway that does not have complicated interchanges or cluttered signage

❑ personally be aware of what is all around.

Make sure your learner:

❑ has read and understood Rules 253-290 of The Highway Code

❑ keeps up with the flow of traffic

❑ uses the Mirrors-Signal-Position-Speed-Look (MSPSL) routine when necessary

❑ uses their planning and awareness skills.

Advanced exercises

Practise:

a on busier motorways

b where there are road works

c on motorway interchanges.

■ End of motorway sign.

Section 8
RAC Advanced Driving Course

This customised training course from RAC is designed to suit any qualified driver who's looking to achieve a higher level of driving skill. You will develop improved driving performance, learn good driving habits and get a real sense of achievement.

A course customised for you

Advanced driving is all about safe and efficient use of road space, as well as developing good driving habits. The RAC Advanced Driving Course has been specially designed to suit any qualified driver who's looking to achieve this higher level of driving skill. It would suit anyone who is looking for a refresher driving course or a high-mileage company car driver who needs to overcome any bad habits that may have developed over the years.

This customised course comprises all the elements you'll need to fully prepare you for the RAC Advanced Driving Test. You'll start with an initial assessment session, which is designed to assess your level of ability for the advanced test.

From this assessment, your training needs will be determined and you'll then have the opportunity to undertake training sessions that are tailored to your individual driving needs. The training will be designed to improve your driving performance and increase your readiness to take the RAC Advanced Driving Test.

Your training car
All sessions should take place in your own car and you'll need to check with your insurer that this is covered on your policy. Using your own car will enable the sessions to be as close to normality as possible, without the added complexity of dealing with a different car.

If you would prefer to use an instructor's vehicle for the sessions, please discuss this at the time of booking.

Specially trained instructors
To give you all the help and support you need, specially selected and trained BSM instructors deliver the advanced training, and the examiner who will take you for your test will be a senior BSM instructor. All our training and

examining is subject to a quality control procedure supervised by Robin Cummins, former Chief Driving Examiner of the Driving Standards Agency.

What the test entails
The test begins with an initial document check and a check of your vehicle to make sure that it appears roadworthy. This is followed by an eyesight check from at least the minimum legal distance given in The Highway Code. You'll then be asked to comment on the type of vehicle you'll be driving and to give an overview of its condition.

The on-road driving test will last approximately 90 minutes, although you should allow a minimum of two hours for the entire test. To reflect varying traffic conditions, test routes will consist of a variety of different road types. Your examiner will ask you to carry out one reversing manoeuvre, either into a parking bay or a side road, and may also include an emergency stop exercise.

At the end of the test, the examiner will ask a minimum of one question on personal safety, vehicle security and environmental issues, and one other from the range of pre-set questions.

Risk-based test assessment
The RAC Advanced Driving Test is assessed using risk and hazard perception and not driving faults. A risk is normally assessed where you put yourself or another road user at risk, or increase the chance of a crash happening. They are assessed at three levels: low risk, significant risk and high risk.

❑ **A low risk** is where a situation is judged not to involve any danger or potential danger.

❑ **A significant risk** is where a situation is judged to have caused unnecessary inconvenience or to involve some potential danger. A significant risk may be recorded where a driving pattern or style is unacceptable.

☐ **A high risk** involves a misjudgement that caused actual danger.

Any significant or high risks that are recorded will result in a failure, as they would on a DSA driving test.

Your examiner will assess the risk element of the circumstances throughout the test. You'll be assessed on your capabilities in managing risk in a variety of different and constantly changing road and traffic conditions. At the end of the test, the examiner will talk you through the assessment, providing balanced and detailed feedback on your performance.

Book your Advanced Driving Course
Ask your BSM instructor for details, contact us at BSM on 08457 276 276* or book your RAC Advanced Driving Course online at www.rac.co.uk

* Calls may be recorded and/or monitored.

Conclusion

There is never a conclusion to learning to drive because there will always be more to learn. Even those who have been driving for many years experience new scenarios and situations on the road.

It is important to build a solid base through good professional instruction and taking plenty of practice on all types of roads and conditions. Taking further training, such as Pass Plus, can enhance your skills, but you must not let this lead to a feeling of over-confidence and immortality. All drivers are vulnerable and liable to lapses of concentration.

Statistically, as a new driver you are at risk on the road. However, a structured learning programme as shown in this book, combined with the right attitude, should enable you to enjoy your new-found freedom safely.

In time, you may find further (advanced) training useful, especially if you are driving a lot of miles per year. For information about these BSM courses and the RAC Advanced test check out www.bsm.co.uk and www.rac.co.uk.

Robin Cummins OBE
Road Safety Consultant

Section 9
Private practice record

On the following pages we have laid out a record block for each of the 45 key skills to be practised with your accompanying driver, with a note of the pages in the book where the skill appears. There are up to 5 records per skill to fill in – 5 blanks are left at the end and if you require more, copy the details on another sheet and keep it together with this book. Circle the number of the practice (Sess. No.), enter the date and circle any of the Advanced exercises practised during the session. Finally, make a note of the time spent on each practice session. Use the filled in example block below as a guide.

Example:

Skill 4	Moving off safely		pages 33–35
Sess. No.	**Date**	**Advanced exercises**	**Time spent practising**
①	14 /08 /2007	a ⓑ c d	2 hours 45 minutes
②	31 /01 /2008	a ⓑ ⓒ ⓓ	One and a half hours
3	/ /	a b c d	
4	/ /	a b c d	
5	/ /	a b c d	

Practice records:

Skill 1	The cockpit drill		pages 26–28
Sess. No.	**Date**	**Advanced exercises**	**Time spent practising**
1	/ /	none suggested	
2	/ /		
3	/ /		
4	/ /		
5	/ /		

Skill 2	Use of car controls and instruments		pages 29–31
Sess. No.	**Date**	**Advanced exercises**	**Time spent practising**
1	/ /	none suggested	
2	/ /		
3	/ /		
4	/ /		
5	/ /		

Skill 3	Controlling the clutch		page 32
Sess. No.	**Date**	**Advanced exercises**	**Time spent practising**
1	/ /	none suggested	
2	/ /		
3	/ /		
4	/ /		
5	/ /		

Skill 4	Moving off safely		pages 33–35
Sess. No.	**Date**	**Advanced exercises**	**Time spent practising**
1	/ /	a b c d	
2	/ /	a b c d	
3	/ /	a b c d	
4	/ /	a b c d	
5	/ /	a b c d	

Skill 5	Moving off at an angle		pages 35–37
Sess. No.	**Date**	**Advanced exercises**	**Time spent practising**
1	/ /	a b c	
2	/ /	a b c	
3	/ /	a b c	
4	/ /	a b c	
5	/ /	a b c	

Skill 6	Moving off uphill		pages 38–39
Sess. No.	**Date**	**Advanced exercises**	**Time spent practising**
1	/ /	none suggested	
2	/ /		
3	/ /		
4	/ /		
5	/ /		

Skill 7	Moving off downhill		pages 40–41
Sess. No.	**Date**	**Advanced exercises**	**Time spent practising**
1	/ /	a b c d e	
2	/ /	a b c d e	
3	/ /	a b c d e	
4	/ /	a b c d e	
5	/ /	a b c d e	

Skill 8	Changing gear		pages 42–43
Sess. No.	**Date**	**Advanced exercises**	**Time spent practising**
1	/ /	a b c	
2	/ /	a b c	
3	/ /	a b c	
4	/ /	a b c	
5	/ /	a b c	

Skill 9	Steering		pages 44–45
Sess. No.	**Date**	**Advanced exercises**	**Time spent practising**
1	/ /	off–road centre or	
2	/ /	BSM simulator	
3	/ /	recommended	
4	/ /		
5	/ /		

Skill 10	Stopping normally		pages 46–47
Sess. No.	**Date**	**Advanced exercises**	**Time spent practising**
1	/ /	none suggested	
2	/ /		
3	/ /		
4	/ /		
5	/ /		

Skill 11	Controlled (emergency) stop		pages 47–48
Sess. No.	**Date**	**Advanced exercises**	**Time spent practising**
1	/ /	none suggested	
2	/ /		
3	/ /		
4	/ /		
5	/ /		

Skill 12	Using the mirrors effectively		pages 49–50
Sess. No.	Date	Advanced exercises	Time spent practising
1	/ /	a b c d	
2	/ /	a b c d	
3	/ /	a b c d	
4	/ /	a b c d	
5	/ /	a b c d	

Skill 13	Giving signals		pages 51–53
Sess. No.	Date	Advanced exercises	Time spent practising
1	/ /	a b c	
2	/ /	a b c	
3	/ /	a b c	
4	/ /	a b c	
5	/ /	a b c	

Skill 14	Acting on signs and signals		pages 53–56
Sess. No.	Date	Advanced exercises	Time spent practising
1	/ /	none suggested	
2	/ /		
3	/ /		
4	/ /		
5	/ /		

Skill 15	Turning left		pages 56–59
Sess. No.	Date	Advanced exercises	Time spent practising
1	/ /	a b c d e	
2	/ /	a b c d e	
3	/ /	a b c d e	
4	/ /	a b c d e	
5	/ /	a b c d e	

Skill 16	Emerging left		pages 60–62
Sess. No.	Date	Advanced exercises	Time spent practising
1	/ /	a b c d e f g	
2	/ /	a b c d e f g	
3	/ /	a b c d e f g	
4	/ /	a b c d e f g	
5	/ /	a b c d e f g	

Skill 17	Turning right		pages 62–64
Sess. No.	Date	Advanced exercises	Time spent practising
1	/ /	a b c d e f	
2	/ /	a b c d e f	
3	/ /	a b c d e f	
4	/ /	a b c d e f	
5	/ /	a b c d e f	

Skill 18	Emerging right		pages 65–67
Sess. No.	Date	Advanced exercises	Time spent practising
1	/ /	a b c d e f g	
2	/ /	a b c d e f g	
3	/ /	a b c d e f g	
4	/ /	a b c d e f g	
5	/ /	a b c d e f g	

Skill 19	Approaching crossroads		pages 67–70
Sess. No.	Date	Advanced exercises	Time spent practising
1	/ /	a b c	
2	/ /	a b c	
3	/ /	a b c	
4	/ /	a b c	
5	/ /	a b c	

Skill 20	Roundabouts		pages 70–73
Sess. No.	Date	Advanced exercises	Time spent practising
1	/ /	a b c d	
2	/ /	a b c d	
3	/ /	a b c d	
4	/ /	a b c d	
5	/ /	a b c d	

Skill 21	Complex junctions		pages 74–75
Sess. No.	Date	Advanced exercises	Time spent practising
1	/ /	a b c	
2	/ /	a b c	
3	/ /	a b c	
4	/ /	a b c	
5	/ /	a b c	

Skill 22	Pedestrian crossings		pages 76–79
Sess. No.	**Date**	**Advanced exercises**	**Time spent practising**
1	/ /	a b c	
2	/ /	a b c	
3	/ /	a b c	
4	/ /	a b c	
5	/ /	a b c	

Skill 23	Level crossings		pages 80–81
Sess. No.	**Date**	**Advanced exercises**	**Time spent practising**
1	/ /	none suggested	
2	/ /		
3	/ /		
4	/ /		
5	/ /		

Skill 24	Keeping space either side		pages 81–82
Sess. No.	**Date**	**Advanced exercises**	**Time spent practising**
1	/ /	a b c	
2	/ /	a b c	
3	/ /	a b c	
4	/ /	a b c	
5	/ /	a b c	

Skill 25	Following traffic		pages 83–85
Sess. No.	**Date**	**Advanced exercises**	**Time spent practising**
1	/ /	a b	
2	/ /	a b	
3	/ /	a b	
4	/ /	a b	
5	/ /	a b	

Skill 26	Keeping pace with traffic		pages 86–87
Sess. No.	**Date**	**Advanced exercises**	**Time spent practising**
1	/ /	a b c	
2	/ /	a b c	
3	/ /	a b c	
4	/ /	a b c	
5	/ /	a b c	

Skill 27   Meeting traffic   pages 87–89

Sess. No.	Date	Advanced exercises	Time spent practising
1	/ /	a b	
2	/ /	a b	
3	/ /	a b	
4	/ /	a b	
5	/ /	a b	

Skill 28   Crossing traffic   pages 89–91

Sess. No.	Date	Advanced exercises	Time spent practising
1	/ /	a b	
2	/ /	a b	
3	/ /	a b	
4	/ /	a b	
5	/ /	a b	

Skill 29   Overtaking   pages 91–93

Sess. No.	Date	Advanced exercises	Time spent practising
1	/ /	a b	
2	/ /	a b	
3	/ /	a b	
4	/ /	a b	
5	/ /	a b	

Skill 30   Awareness and planning – towns   pages 94–97

Sess. No.	Date	Advanced exercises	Time spent practising
1	/ /	a b c	
2	/ /	a b c	
3	/ /	a b c	
4	/ /	a b c	
5	/ /	a b c	

Skill 31   Awareness and planning – country roads   pages 98–99

Sess. No.	Date	Advanced exercises	Time spent practising
1	/ /	a b	
2	/ /	a b	
3	/ /	a b	
4	/ /	a b	
5	/ /	a b	

Skill 32   Lane discipline and positioning   pages 100–102

Sess. No.	Date	Advanced exercises	Time spent practising
1	/ /	a b	
2	/ /	a b	
3	/ /	a b	
4	/ /	a b	
5	/ /	a b	

Skill 33   One–way systems   pages 103–105

Sess. No.	Date	Advanced exercises	Time spent practising
1	/ /	a b	
2	/ /	a b	
3	/ /	a b	
4	/ /	a b	
5	/ /	a b	

Skill 34   Dual carriageways   pages 106–108

Sess. No.	Date	Advanced exercises	Time spent practising
1	/ /	a b c d	
2	/ /	a b c d	
3	/ /	a b c d	
4	/ /	a b c d	
5	/ /	a b c d	

Skill 35   Eco–friendly driving   pages 109–110

Sess. No.	Date	Advanced exercises	Time spent practising
1	/ /	a b	
2	/ /	a b	
3	/ /	a b	
4	/ /	a b	
5	/ /	a b	

Skill 36   Night driving   pages 111–115

Sess. No.	Date	Advanced exercises	Time spent practising
1	/ /	a b c	
2	/ /	a b c	
3	/ /	a b c	
4	/ /	a b c	
5	/ /	a b c	

Skill 37	Bad weather		pages 116–118
Sess. No.	**Date**	**Advanced exercises**	**Time spent practising**
1	/ /	a b	
2	/ /	a b	
3	/ /	a b	
4	/ /	a b	
5	/ /	a b	

Skill 38	Commentary driving		pages 119–120
Sess. No.	**Date**	**Advanced exercises**	**Time spent practising**
1	/ /	a b c d	
2	/ /	a b c d	
3	/ /	a b c d	
4	/ /	a b c d	
5	/ /	a b c d	

Skill 39	Reversing in a straight line		pages 121–123
Sess. No.	**Date**	**Advanced exercises**	**Time spent practising**
1	/ /	none suggested	
2	/ /		
3	/ /		
4	/ /		
5	/ /		

Skill 40	Sharp left reverse		pages 123–126
Sess. No.	**Date**	**Advanced exercises**	**Time spent practising**
1	/ /	a b c	
2	/ /	a b c	
3	/ /	a b c	
4	/ /	a b c	
5	/ /	a b c	

Skill 41	Sweeping left reverse		pages 126–127
Sess. No.	**Date**	**Advanced exercises**	**Time spent practising**
1	/ /	a b c	
2	/ /	a b c	
3	/ /	a b c	
4	/ /	a b c	
5	/ /	a b c	

Skill 42	Reverse to the right		pages 128–131
Sess. No.	Date	Advanced exercises	Time spent practising
1	/ /	a b c d e	
2	/ /	a b c d e	
3	/ /	a b c d e	
4	/ /	a b c d e	
5	/ /	a b c d e	

Skill 43	Turn in the road		pages 131–135
Sess. No.	Date	Advanced exercises	Time spent practising
1	/ /	a b c d e	
2	/ /	a b c d e	
3	/ /	a b c d e	
4	/ /	a b c d e	
5	/ /	a b c d e	

Skill 44	Reverse park		pages 135–138
Sess. No.	Date	Advanced exercises	Time spent practising
1	/ /	a b c d e	
2	/ /	a b c d e	
3	/ /	a b c d e	
4	/ /	a b c d e	
5	/ /	a b c d e	

Skill 45	Reversing into a bay		pages 139–141
Sess. No.	Date	Advanced exercises	Time spent practising
1	/ /	a b c d e	
2	/ /	a b c d e	
3	/ /	a b c d e	
4	/ /	a b c d e	
5	/ /	a b c d e	

Motorways (after passing the Practical Test)			pages 157–162
Sess. No.	Date	Advanced exercises	Time spent practising
1	/ /	a b c	
2	/ /	a b c	
3	/ /	a b c	
4	/ /	a b c	
5	/ /	a b c	

Blank practice records:

Skill____ Subject_____

Sess. No.	Date	Advanced exercises	Time spent practising
1	/ /	a b c d e f g	
2	/ /	a b c d e f g	
3	/ /	a b c d e f g	
4	/ /	a b c d e f g	
5	/ /	a b c d e f g	

Skill____ Subject_____

Sess. No.	Date	Advanced exercises	Time spent practising
1	/ /	a b c d e f g	
2	/ /	a b c d e f g	
3	/ /	a b c d e f g	
4	/ /	a b c d e f g	
5	/ /	a b c d e f g	

Skill____ Subject_____

Sess. No.	Date	Advanced exercises	Time spent practising
1	/ /	a b c d e f g	
2	/ /	a b c d e f g	
3	/ /	a b c d e f g	
4	/ /	a b c d e f g	
5	/ /	a b c d e f g	

Skill____ Subject_____

Sess. No.	Date	Advanced exercises	Time spent practising
1	/ /	a b c d e f g	
2	/ /	a b c d e f g	
3	/ /	a b c d e f g	
4	/ /	a b c d e f g	
5	/ /	a b c d e f g	

Skill____ Subject_____

Sess. No.	Date	Advanced exercises	Time spent practising
1	/ /	a b c d e f g	
2	/ /	a b c d e f g	
3	/ /	a b c d e f g	
4	/ /	a b c d e f g	
5	/ /	a b c d e f g	